RADIO AND ELECTRIC POWER SUPPLY EQUIPMENT FOR SCHOOLS

BY

EDWARD CHARLES BLOM, Ph.D.

TEACHERS COLLEGE, COLUMBIA UNIVERSITY
CONTRIBUTIONS TO EDUCATION, No. 409

BUREAU OF PUBLICATIONS

Teachers College, Columbia University

NEW YORK CITY

1930

ACKNOWLEDGMENTS

The author desires to acknowledge his indebtedness to Professors N. L. Engelhardt and S. R. Powers for suggesting the two parts of the problem and for their constant assistance and encouragement during the prosecution of the study. To Professors George D. Strayer, F. W. Johnson, Paul R. Mort, Carter Alexander, and Willard S. Elsbree, and to many graduate students of Teachers College he wishes to acknowledge the useful and stimulating suggestions they have so generously contributed.

For much of the technical information needed in this study the author is indebted to many specialists associated with manufacturers of radio and electric power supply equipment. He is deeply grateful to representatives of the Radio Corporation of America, Stromberg-Carlson Company, Graybar Electric Company, General Electric Company, Westinghouse Lamp Company, as well as to Professor W. A. Curry and Mr. W. W. Macalpine of Columbia University for their criticism of parts of the manuscript. To Dr. H. C. Rentschler, the author is particularly grateful for his criticism of the entire manuscript.

Finally, the author is profoundly indebted to his wife, Mrs. E. Alice Blom, for her whole-hearted coöperation and assistance throughout the entire study.

E. C. B.

CONTENTS

PART I

RADIO AND ALLIED EQUIPMENT FOR SCHOOLS

PART II

ELECTRIC POWER SUPPLY FOR HIGH SCHOOL SCIENCE ROOMS

PART I

RADIO AND ALLIED EQUIPMENT
FOR SCHOOLS

INTRODUCTION

Certain kinds of electrical equipment have been in use in schools for sufficiently long periods to have become somewhat standardized. Equipment for the fire alarm system, program system, clock system, telephone system, and lighting system, as well as many kinds of motor-driven machinery, are examples. Manufacturers of electrical equipment are making new developments constantly. As these new developments are placed upon the market the school officials must judge their merits as related to the needs of the school. Where reasonably satisfactory standards are available, the difficulty encountered in making selections is considerably reduced.

This study deals with electrical equipment used for instructional purposes. The particular kinds of equipment considered are those associated with (1) school radio installations, and (2) electric power supply for high school science rooms. Knowledge regarding the electric equipment needs for these services is not readily available at the present time. In general, the manufacturers do not know what the school needs are and the educational administrators are unable to furnish the necessary information. In the case of radio equipment for schools, educational administrators are not sufficiently familiar with what the trade has to offer, largely because radio has been used in connection with school work for only a short time. Concerning the fixed equipment associated with power supply for science rooms, the primary trouble has been lack of knowledge of the actual power requirement for work carried on in these rooms.

This study purposes furnishing school administrators with information to guide them in selecting equipment and in placing installations, and informing the manufacturers of the needs of the schools which their products must satisfy.

For both the radio equipment and the power supply equipment, data were obtained through interviews, by the use of questionnaires, from the study of plans and specifications, and from the analysis of published literature.

3

Because of the contemporary nature of this study, as far as radio equipment is concerned, the author was unable to obtain information from many educators who had had experience with this type of equipment. Technical information was obtained from published literature and from many interviews with radio specialists working in research laboratories, technical laboratories, and sales departments. The author interviewed specialists employed by commercial firms and two radio specialists who are professors at Columbia University.

Data related to the electric power supply for physics, chemistry, biology, and general science rooms were obtained from several different sources, with the idea in mind of eliminating biases. Science teachers of forty large high schools in New York, New Jersey, Connecticut, Pennsylvania, and Massachusetts were interviewed while the author was visiting these schools to inspect the equipment actually used. Other interviews were obtained with engineers specializing in laboratory power supply equipment, professors who train science teachers, research workers, apparatus salesmen, and school building engineers. Courses of study, textbooks, and laboratory manuals were studied to learn what power supply is necessary to carry on the work outlined. Lists of required and recommended equipment for science laboratories were checked, and the characteristics of equipment listed were determined from a study of several apparatus catalogues. Letters including a questionnaire were sent to the heads of science departments or to some other outstanding science teachers in each of twenty large cities. These teachers were asked to supply the names of other teachers who would, they believed, be willing and qualified to answer this questionnaire. Questionnaires were then sent to the persons whose names had been supplied. From this selected group, thirty-four replies were received. The cities represented are New York, Chicago, Philadelphia, Detroit, Cleveland, St. Louis, Denver, Minneapolis, Milwaukee, St. Paul, Pittsburgh, Washington, New Orleans, Cambridge (Mass.), Gardner (Mass.), and Shippensburg (Pa.).

The method of treating the data is primarily analytical. Information gathered from the various sources was analyzed and interpreted. Judgments of educators who have had experience with the several types of electrical equipment studied were combined with opinions of technical experts to determine the provisions necessary to meet school needs. From the study of needs and ways of meeting these needs, lists of desirable characteristics of each major item of equipment were developed. These lists were submitted to experts for criticism. Statements which were considered questionable or of little importance were omitted from the final lists. With due consideration of the educational implications and technical difficulties involved, several installations were suggested for both the radio equipment and the power supply equipment. These suggested installations vary in elaborateness, the idea being to provide for minimum requirements as revealed by this study and, at the same time, to allow considerable freedom of choice where elaborateness is concerned.

This study does not pretend to give final solutions for the problems connected with school radio and power supply equipment, but rather to offer solutions on the basis of conditions as they now exist, and in accordance with probable future developments. Researches in the fields of radio, television, and tone pictures will doubtless result in new developments, the influence of which will be felt in the schools.

CHAPTER I

THE USE OF RADIO AND ALLIED SERVICES
IN SCHOOLS

The purpose of this chapter is to point out some of the important considerations relative to the use of radio and allied services in schools. The allied services include devices for amplifying and distributing music and speech. This chapter deals with the following major topics: (1) some trends in the use of radio in schools; (2) experiences of some educators who have used radio and allied services in school work; (3) sources of programs; (4) some important considerations in determining the advisability of installing radio equipment in schools; and (5) the desirable over-all characteristics which a radio installation should possess.

SOME TRENDS IN THE USE OF RADIO AND
ALLIED SERVICES IN SCHOOLS

Within the past year an increasing amount of interest has been shown on the part of educators in the use of radio and allied services as aids to instruction.

In some of the foreign countries serious consideration is being given to the use of educational broadcasting in connection with the work of the schools. The recent action of the Swedish Board of Education is one of the best examples. The following clipping indicates what is being done in Sweden:

Stockholm, March 2, 1929. Radio has now invaded Swedish schools. After a series of extensive tests conducted in April last year, the Swedish Board of Education, in connection with the government-owned broadcasting service, has announced a series of lectures to be given by leading writers, pedagogues, etc. These will be relayed to all schools equipped with receiving equipment.

The program dealing with history, geography, foreign languages, etc., will be put on the air four times a week for a half hour each. If the lessons are well received by the majority of schools they will become permanent features of the national broadcasting service.

Many renowned authors have promised to coöperate. The programs will be sent from the new studios of the Stockholm broadcasting station.[1]

The British Broadcasting Company is undertaking systematic investigations in the use of broadcasting in connection with school work. Since favorable results were obtained from the Kent County [2] experiments, the British Broadcasting Company has set up a central council for school broadcasting. This council is proceeding to deal with the specific problem of broadcasting to schools. A copy of the summary of the recommendations and suggestions contained in the report of the Kent experiment appears in Appendix D.

Probably the most convincing evidence of interest on the part of the schools of our own country in a well-planned educational program is the response given to the Damrosch concerts broadcast by the National Broadcasting Company. Each chain station was asked to send questionnaires to every school in its district to ascertain the number of children hearing the concerts. Returns received after the first concert indicated that children in 44,000 schools had listened in. The success of this undertaking is probably the outgrowth of the great care which was exercised in planning the programs and in providing instructional aids to accompany them. The programs were arranged with the aid of an advisory council and a large advisory committee composed of school superintendents and music supervisors. There is every reason to believe that what has been done in this way in music will be extended to many other subjects.

On May 24, 1929 a radio education conference was held in Washington, D.C., at the invitation of Secretary Wilbur. At this conference a resolution was passed asking President Hoover to appoint a fact-finding commission to ascertain what radio can do for education, and the part the Federal Government should play in any such program of education.

Miss Ida M. Baker is now conducting an experiment on the use of radio in the teaching of arithmetic to 300 children in eight rooms in the 2A and 3B grades of the Tremont School, Cleveland, Ohio. According to the teachers and supervisors who work in this school the results justify the following conclusions:

[1] *New York Herald Tribune,* March 3, 1929.

[2] "Educational Broadcasting." *Report of a Special Investigation in the County of Kent During the Year 1927.* The Carnegie United Kingdom Trustees, Comely Park House, Dunfermline, 1928.

1. The impersonality of the device has focused the attention of both teachers and pupils on the learning process.

2. It has given the teachers a new enthusiasm for scientific planning of all lessons, and has drawn the teachers more closely together in the spirit of friendly and helpful criticism.

3. It seems to be possible to measure the results accurately and scientifically and to substitute exact knowledge of the child's learning ability for guesswork and rule-of-thumb methods.[3]

The fact that experiments of this kind are in progress indicates that serious consideration is being given to the use of radio for instructional purposes.

SOURCES OF PROGRAMS

One of the greatest troubles in the past has been to get the schools and the broadcasters together. From a purely economical standpoint it is reasonable to expect that the large chain broadcasters will look with favor upon the educational programs for schools because these programs will be given during those hours of the day when the traffic for these stations is low. That the large broadcasting companies are interested in furnishing suitable educational programs is indicated in an Associated Press article which appeared in the *New York Herald Tribune* on April 20, 1929. This article stated that heads of the National Broadcasting Company and the Columbia chain executives have informed the United States Bureau of Education that they would welcome its coöperation in working out a real course of study for the radio to synchronize as far as possible with the standard subjects used in the schools. If the experiments with short waves for international broadcasting prove successful another large supply of programs will be available. The use of short waves may make broadcasting within the United States more economical because of the elimination of wire tolls.

The large national broadcasting stations are not the only sources from which educational programs can be obtained. Nearly every section of the United States has at least one good local commercial station. In addition to the commercial stations there are the stations operated by large universities and colleges. Extensive broadcasting is done by some of the state schools like Kansas State Agricultural College, Iowa State Col-

[3] "Radio Lessons Put Penalty on Guessing." *School Topics*, Vol. XI, No. 14, April 9, 1929.

lege of Agriculture and Mechanic Arts, South Dakota State College of Agriculture and Mechanic Arts, Ohio State University, and the State University of Iowa. These schools include in their programs material suitable to supplement the work of elementary and secondary schools. The published programs of the Kansas State Agricultural College indicate that daily programs of twenty-five minutes are intended for rural schools.

Some state departments of education such as those for Connecticut and Ohio have used broadcasting in carrying out their work. The Ohio State Educational Department enlisted radio to broadcast a series of lectures for school teachers. On March 16, 1929, Governor Graves of Alabama announced that radio would be used in an endeavor to expand the state's educational program.

In Fort Bend County, Texas, the County School Board recently placed in operation its own broadcasting plant. The plant serves thirty-six rural schools and four institutions in Richmond, Texas and Rosenberg, Texas.

The WODA Free Grammar and High School of the Air located at Paterson, New Jersey, is an illustration of an institution using radio as the principal medium for the presentation of subject matter. Among the subjects offered by this institution are English composition, grammar, algebra, arithmetic, general science, social science, anthropology, history, agriculture, nature study, drama, and home economics. In a letter dated February 27, 1929, Mr. Ellsworth Tompkins, program manager, informed the author that 1,112 listeners had enrolled in the school to date.

Broadcasting within a school system offers another, and by no means the least important, source of programs. This kind of broadcasting offers an unusual opportunity for local initiative.

EXPERIENCES OF EDUCATORS WHO HAVE USED RADIO AND ALLIED SERVICES IN SCHOOL WORK

The purpose of this section is to point out some of the problems which confront the educator in the use of radio and speech and music amplification systems, as well as to show how specific problems are now handled and what those who have actually worked in this field believe relative to future trends. It is true that some of the outstanding problems can never be solved by simply furnishing the teacher with equipment with which to work. If a new kind of equipment is furnished then the teacher must learn how to use it most effectively. There is no question that the use of radio as an aid in education will require special teaching techniques if the best results are to be obtained. Mr. T. E. Spencer, director, Reference Research and Publicity, St. Louis Public Schools, pointed out other problems which must be solved when he said:

> The full use of radio broadcasting as an educational means must wait upon the installation of radio receiving sets and amplifiers generally throughout the schoolrooms, but, more particularly, must wait upon the organization of educational agencies whose effect can be produced by such means.[4]

Inquiries concerning the use of radio equipment were sent to a small and carefully selected group. This was done because the use of radio and public address equipment in schools is of such recent origin that most schoolmen have not had much experience with it. In response to a questionnaire distributed to a group of experienced superintendents and principals in Teachers College, Columbia University, thirty-eight replies were obtained. Only four of those replying indicated that any kind of radio or public address equipment was being used in their schools. Since this group of men represented many cities of different sizes located in different parts of the United States, it was deemed advisable to direct further inquiries to people who had actually used the equipment. Those people would be in a position to supply more reliable information of value in determining what should be included in a desirable set-up.

Those who have actually worked with radio equipment in schools favor the use of a central station with loud speakers in every room. Mr. Glenn H. Woods, director of Music, Oakland Public Schools, says:

> Very soon after the radio was commercialized, the Oakland schools started a program of radio education. We experimented on giving instruction by radio in almost every school subject. The lack of equipment made it almost impossible to carry on this activity with a sufficient degree of success to warrant its further development. . . . I would favor a central receiving set with loud speakers for each room. . . . I should however, at present be happy to have a good receiving set in each school, and use it in the auditorium. This is less expensive and can reach at least those groups that are interested in particular subjects and particular broadcasts.[5]

[4] Letter to the author, November 28, 1928.
[5] Letter to the author, November 24, 1928.

Considerable use has been made of radio by the Division of Rural Education of the Connecticut State Board of Education. Mr. N. Searle Light, director, Division of Rural Education, Connecticut State Department of Education, has been directing the work in Connecticut. He says, "We are advising the installation of the central receiving set in all schools of two or more rooms." [6]

It is interesting to have the opinion of one who prepares and directs educational programs for a large broadcasting station. Mr. Harold O. Totter says:

. . . the ideal equipment and the thing I believe we will come to eventually, will be a set or possibly two sets in a school operated from some central source with the rooms wired for speakers so that the pupils can receive the programs in their rooms and in smaller groups, which is more satisfactory.[7]

Superintendent L. G. Jones of the Cleveland, Ohio, schools informed the writer that the experiments now being carried on at Tremont School in teaching arithmetic with the use of a centralized radio system are giving results sufficiently satisfactory to warrant investigating the possibilities of providing some kind of connection between different schools or probably all the schools of the same grade so that a given lesson would reach a very large number of children in their own classrooms. It is apparent that Dr. Jones favors the use of centralized systems for school work. Miss Ida M. Baker, who is conducting the experiment referred to above, said:

We have had excellent results from the panel system (audio frequency distribution system), no static, and a clear voice. Very few children miss the examples because they do not hear the directions or the dictated numbers.[8]

The following questions were asked the principals of schools in which central distribution systems of some kind had been in use for a long enough period for the operating characteristics to be known. Tables 1-A, 1-B, and 1-C give the results of this inquiry.

QUESTIONS

1. Check the kinds of service which your system provided (a) radio reception...... (b) close talking (regular telephone transmitter)...... (c) broadcasting microphone..... (d) electric phonograph pickup.....

[6] Personal letter to the author, November 19, 1928.
[7] Director of Educational Programs, WMAQ, Radio Station of the *Chicago Daily News*. Letter to the author, November 16, 1928.
[8] Letter to the author, April 23, 1929.

2. Which, if any, of the above are unsatisfactory?........................

3. Which, if any, are not needed?.....................................

4. Rank the services in order of importance.............................

5. Are the loud speakers permanently mounted on the wall?............

6. In what places in the building are loud speakers located?.............

....

7. Who supervises the system?..

8. Have you experienced trouble through damage to the loud speakers or theft of parts?.......................,...............................

9. What have been your principal maintenance or operation troubles?....

....

10. Do you believe that there is need for receiving more than one program at a time?..

11. In what ways do you believe the service could be made more valuable to the school?...

Not one principal who has attempted to use radio as a means of instruction reported favoring individual sets more than the centralized equipment, provided the school could afford the

TABLE 1-A

INPUT SERVICES FOR PUBLIC ADDRESS AND RADIO SYSTEMS

Replies to Questionnaire

School Number	Kind of Input Services Furnished				Unsatis-factory Input	Unnec-essary Input	Input Equip-ment Ranked in Order of Im-portance	Is There Need for More Than One Program at a Time?
	Radio Re-ceiver (a)	Close-Talking Tele-phone (b)	Broad-casting Micro-phone (c)	Phono-graph Pickup (d)				
1	x		x	x	None		C-A-D	No
2		x	x		None	None	Equal	No
3		x						No
4	x	x	x	x	None	None	C-A-D-B	No
5	x		x					No
6	x	x	x	x	None	None	B-A-C-D	No
7	x							No
8	x			x			A	No
9	x		x		None	None	C-A	No
10		x	x		None	None	A-B-C	Probably
11	x				Recep-tion			Yes
12	x		x	x	None	None	A-D-C	Yes
13	x		x	x				No
14	x		x	x	None	None	A	Probably

TABLE 1-B

LOCATION AND MANNER OF MOUNTING LOUD SPEAKERS

Replies to Questionnaire

School Number	Are Loud Speakers Mounted Permanently on the Wall?	Places Where Loud Speaker Outlets are Located					
		All Class-rooms	Audito-rium or Assembly	Cafeteria or Din-ing Hall	Gym-nasium	Out-of-Doors	Other Places
1	Yes		x				
2	Yes	x					
3	Yes		x				
4	Yes		x				
5	Some		x		x	x	x
6	Yes	x	x	x			
7	No						
8	No	x	x				x
9	Yes		x				
10	Yes	x	x		x		
11	No	x			x		
12	No	x	x				x
13	Yes			x			
14	No	x	x		x		

latter. Moreover, only four out of fourteen principals believed that provision need be made for the reception of two or more programs simultaneously. In the present installations, radio reception and voice extension (broadcast microphone input) are most common and are considered most important also by principals. In all cases where these services were available they were considered necessary and no distinct advantage of one over the other was claimed, nor was one favored more than the other. In some situations where the acoustic properties of a room were bad or where the room was very large the voice extension (microphone service) facilities were practically a necessity. Mr. R. B. Leland, principal of the senior high school, San Jose, California, said, "We have found that the use of the public address system has added intensely to the interest of students in public programs of every character." In no case did the principal feel that some of the services furnished in his installation were not needed.

There is no uniformity in the placement of responsibility for supervision and operation of the central station equipment. The

TABLE 1-C

SUPERVISION AND MAINTENANCE OF RADIO AND PUBLIC ADDRESS EQUIPMENT

Replies to Questionnaire

SCHOOL NUMBER	PERSONS SUPERVISING THE SYSTEM					DAMAGE TO LOUD SPEAKER OR LOSS OF PARTS	MAINTENANCE AND OPERATION TROUBLES
	Superintendent and Assistants	Principal and Assistants	Electrician or Custodian	Teacher	Teacher and Students		
1					x	None	None
2		x				None	None
3		x	x			--	Microphone
4				x		None	None
5			x			Theft	None
6		x				None	None
7		x				None	None
8		x				None	None
9					x	None	Cleaning
10				x		Theft	Batteries
11		x	x			None	None
12		x				None	--
13				x		None	None
14	x					None	None

principal and his office assistants assume this responsibility in most cases. Frequently the school electrician is in charge. In some cases a science teacher, manual arts teacher, or the teacher in charge of the stage will care for this equipment, usually with the aid of a student. In one case the radio club of the school took full responsibility for supervision and operation of the equipment.

The reports indicate that in most cases where centralized equipment is in use the loud speakers are permanently mounted on the walls. In seven of these buildings all of the classrooms were wired for loud speakers. Many of the new buildings are now being wired so that a loud speaker can be placed in every room. In some cases the equipment itself has not been installed but provisions have been made in the original wiring for installing the equipment at some future time. When loud speaker outlets are provided in the classrooms they are usually placed on the front wall. It is a common practice to have loud speakers in the front of the auditorium either as clusters above or as individual units at the sides of the stage opening. When speakers are located in gymnasiums they are placed in positions where there is little danger of injury, as on the side walls. Sometimes the speakers are placed on the wall which separates the locker room from the gymnasium. In some cases the acoustic properties of the gymnasiums are corrected in order that the loud speaker may be heard easily. In practically all the new buildings and in some of the old ones, loud speakers are located in the cafeterias. The installation at the Columbia High School, South Orange, New Jersey, includes provisions for loud speaker service outside at the rear of the building.

In all cases it has been found advisable to make every reasonable provision to prevent theft of parts. Two loud speakers were stolen from one building during the summer months while an addition was under construction. In other cases various parts were stolen. The maintenance problems in most cases were very simple, in fact the only real trouble reported was that the batteries required a great deal of attention.

Suggestions were made by some of the principals relative to ways in which their installations could be made more valuable to the school. In every case where radio was not included in the original installation the principal stated that this service was needed. Mr. E. L. Burton, principal of the Webster Junior High School, Oklahoma City, Oklahoma, said, "Let all future announcements be as explicit and early-dated as the present Damrosch concerts, bulletined by Radio Corporation of America." Several of those who replied were of the opinion that the service could be more valuable if state departments of education or some other responsible organization would establish broadcasting stations for educational programs during school hours. Mr. George Sype, principal of Lawson School, Chicago, believes that more programs should be given in the afternoon and that clearer enunciation on the part of some of the speakers would be desirable. In the following statement Mr. Sype shows what can be done to meet a given situation where ideal provisions have not been made.

We use a portable set and move it from room to room according to class of pupils we wish to reach—fourth, fifth, sixth, seventh, or eighth grades. We put two, three, or four groups or divisions of pupils in one room in order to reach as many pupils of a given grade as possible. We find that room reception for school programs is better for instructional purposes than assembly hall reception. We use the set for assembly hall reception to secure musical accompaniment for educational movies twice a month. We have an aerial (antenna) for assembly hall, and four aerials scattered around the building for room reception. One aerial, by being placed in vertical position, serves three rooms. One centrally located receiver with speakers in all rooms connected electrically with receiver to be turned on at will would be better (though more expensive) than our system.

The experiences of these educators who have used equipment of this kind indicate that:

1. Centralized radio equipment is more desirable than individual sets.

2. Of the four common types of input to a centralized system the radio and broadcasting microphone are more useful than the close-talking telephone and the phonograph. None of these types of service were considered superfluous.

3. Classroom reception of radio programs is better for instructional purposes than assembly hall reception.

4. Adequate provisions must be made to minimize the chances of radio equipment being stolen or damaged.

5. The principal and office assistants usually assume the responsibility of supervising the central station equipment. When an electrician is employed for the building he is often placed in charge of the equipment.

6. The maintenance problems are not significant.

7. Except in very large buildings there is no need for receiving more than two radio programs simultaneously. At present, one program at a time seems to be sufficient.

8. Speech and music amplification systems are valuable in large auditoriums, gymnasiums, and cafeterias. They save considerable time in connection with announcements, short addresses, etc., when loud speakers are located in the classrooms.

9. State departments of education and other educational agencies could aid in supervising and planning educational programs.

10. Broadcast programs should be announced some time before they are given and the teachers should be supplied with instructional materials to be used with the programs.

11. Parent-teacher associations and similar organizations can aid in securing equipment when the necessary funds cannot be obtained from the school treasury.

12. Local broadcasting within the school system seems desirable.

IMPORTANT CONSIDERATIONS IN DETERMINING THE ADVISABILITY
OF INSTALLING RADIO EQUIPMENT IN SCHOOLS

In order to determine whether or not radio should be furnished
as a part of the equipment to be used for instructional purposes,
it is necessary to evaluate the services which a radio installation
can afford. This evaluation should be done from the educator's
point of view. The following are certain considerations which
may serve as bases for evaluation. In developing these statements the procedure was to analyze carefully the purposes of
public education as set forth by prominent educators and to determine how instructional equipment might function to further
these purposes. The experience of educators in the use of instructional equipment was kept in mind constantly. After the
preliminary statements had been formulated, they were submitted to teachers and educational administrators for criticsm.
The following statements concerning radio equipment were then
set up.

1. *Use for Study Purposes.*

In those cases where it is practicable, equipment should be so
installed that the pupils can study its construction and operation.
The relative educational values of installations of all devices
should play a part in the choice of the final installation. The
amount of money spent to make the equipment suitable for educational purposes should be proportionate to educational returns
obtainable. This does not mean that every item of equipment
should be suitable for study purposes.

2. *Noninterference Between Activities.*

The equipment should be so installed that its use in connection
with activities carried on at one place will not cause interference
with other activities carried on at the same time in other places
in the school plant.

3. *Promotion of Economy in Time for Pupils, Teachers, and
Other Workers in the Building.*

The equipment should contribute to minimizing the time required for learning and teaching as well as aid in making the
administrative and other duties more efficient.

4. *Extension of Contacts of the School with the Home and with the World.*

Such facilities should be provided in the school as will make it possible for the child to get in touch with actual life situations as they occur in the home and in the world at large. These facilities should increase the richness, meaning, and accuracy of the child's experiences. Provision should be made to inform the parents and others outside the school of what is being done in the school. Installations which may result in educational isolations are undesirable. It is desirable to employ as educational devices those kinds of equipment which, through their use in life situations, have aroused worth-while interests and enthusiasms in the children.

5. *Provision of Maximum Freedom of the Activities of the Child.*

If full benefit is to be obtained from the natural activities of the children the equipment must be such that the children can use it freely in connection with the particular activities in which they may wish to engage. The arrangements should be adaptable to use with a variety of activities and classroom procedures.

6. *Aid to Supervision of Instruction.*

Equipment which furnishes a means of guiding teachers in improving their own instruction is desirable.

7. *Community Use of the School Buildings.*

Such equipment should be installed as will contribute to making community use of the school building most effective.

8. *Broadening of Educational Offerings.*

Certain kinds of equipment make possible the offering of special courses which cannot be given by the regular teaching staff. Such equipment is desirable if the cost is not prohibitive.

9. *Conformity of Instruments of Instruction to Best Commercial and Industrial Practice.*

The child who is preparing for any particular occupation should use such essential tools and equipment as will conform to the best practice in that field in which the learnings are to be applied.

10. *Definite Educational Aim.*

The installation of radio equipment must be such as to make possible the achievement of definite educational aims as contrasted with entertainment aims. It should aid in providing for explorations and guidance, in imparting knowledge and skills in the fundamental processes, and in achieving a democratic education.

11. *Novelties Not Necessarily Desirable.*

An installation is not necessarily desirable because of the novelty of the enterprise. Devices which are still in the experimental stage should not be chosen.

DESIRABLE OVER-ALL CHARACTERISTICS WHICH A RADIO INSTALLATION SHOULD POSSESS

When the decision has been made that a radio installation is a desirable part of the school equipment, it is necessary to know the important considerations in the selection and installation of this equipment. Important considerations relative to parts of the installation are given at the end of Chapter III; answers to important questions regarding installations are given in Appendix A; and suggested installations are given in Appendix B. Some of the desirable characteristics which apply to the installation as a whole are listed below. These generalizations were formulated after careful consideration of technical problems involved in furnishing those facilities which are suitable for schools. Probable new developments were kept in mind constantly. In developing the statements, care was taken to utilize such information as is given in preceding parts of this chapter and in the chapters which follow.

1. *Safety.*

All items of equipment should be so installed that the chance of injury to people working with or around them is reduced to a minimum. Machines having moving parts should be amply supplied with guards. Every precaution should be taken to eliminate the danger of electrical shocks and burns. Bare terminals should never be left in exposed places. The installations should be such that in their use and study the health of the children will be protected and their safety assured.

2. *Simplicity.*

Simplicity in design and construction consistent with the proper operating conditions should be characteristic of all electrical equipment. It is frequently true that the addition of some service greatly increases the complexity of the mechanism. Complex arrangements should not be employed where simple ones will perform the service equally as well.

3. *Accessibility.*

The items of equipment should be so placed that they are readily accessible to those who must use them. Switches and other controls should be placed so that they can be reached easily. Individual units should be located where they can be used to the best advantage.

4. *Minimum Fire Hazard.*

Unless the proper precautions are taken with electrical installations they are likely to prove fire hazards. All requirements of the National Board of Fire Underwriters and the standards given in the National Electric Code should be adhered to closely.

5. *Ease and Certainty of Operation.*

All equipment intended for general use should be such as can be operated easily by persons who do not have special technical training. Features which minimize the effects of ignorance, carelessness, and forgetfulness are desirable.

6. *Ease of Maintenance.*

Other things being equal, that kind of equipment is to be preferred which is easy to maintain for long periods of continuous service. Should special maintenance service be required, care should be taken that this service is readily available at a reasonable cost.

7. *Standardization of Materials and Equipment.*

Standardization is important from the standpoint of both economy and service. Costly patented features and special designs often have unusual maintenance requirements.

8. *Conservation of Electricity.*

Such installation should be made as will require the minimum waste of electricity consistent with satisfactory service. Electricity should not be conserved if by doing so other more important wastes are incurred. The total electrical equipment may well be greater where electricity is cheap.

9. *Appearance.*

Other things being equal, equipment should be selected which will be pleasing in appearance and which will harmonize with the architecture of the building, and with the other furnishings in the room.

10. *Initial Cost.*

Installations should be made on the basis of utility rather than ornamentation. Nor should quality be sacrificed to economy.

11. *Suitability to Temperature Conditions.*

Proper provisions should be made to meet all ranges and variations in temperature to which the equipment may be subjected under operating conditions.

12. *Suitability to Humidity Conditions.*

Changes of air humidity and extreme humidity conditions should be adequately provided for.

13. *Strength Beyond Maximum Requirements for Operating Conditions.*

The factor of safety beyond the maximum requirements for operating conditions should be allowed for in setting up requirements for the strength of all materials and devices.

14. *Proper Electric Insulation.*

From the standpoint of safety and efficiency of operation it is essential that proper means of insulating be employed.

15. *Proper Grounding.*

In all installations electrical grounding should be adequate. These ground connections should be made so that they will be strong and electrically perfect.

16. *Adequacy.*

Installations should be made so that maximum demands can be met without affecting the quality of the service.

17. *Ease of Cleaning Equipment and Surroundings.*

All installations should be made so that the working parts and the surroundings can be cleaned easily. This is necessary from the standpoint of sanitation, efficiency of operation, and elimination of fire hazards. Dust pockets, pressed and raised ornamentations, and spaces into which waste paper or other refuse can be placed should be avoided.

18. *Adequate Protective Devices.*

All equipment should be protected against mechanical and electrical injury. Wires should be placed in properly supported conduits and all circuits should be adequately fused. Provisions should be made to minimize possible losses due to theft. Flush type loud speakers mounted in the wall are desirable.

19. *Strength and Electrical Soundness of Connections.*

All connections should be sufficiently strong to withstand any mechanical strains placed upon them. They should offer a minimum of resistance to the flow of the electric current.

20. *Durability.*

The equipment and installation should be such as will withstand ordinary abuse and common accidents.

21. *Illumination.*

All installations should be so made that there will be adequate natural or artificial illumination for inspections, repair work, and normal control work.

22. *Ventilation.*

Many items of electrical equipment require free circulation of air around them. In some instances this is necessary to avoid the accumulation of explosive mixtures.

23. *Undesirable Locations.*

Whenever possible, extremely damp locations should be avoided. If equipment must be placed in damp places special provisions must be made in the way of extra waterproof insulation, noncorrosive and nonabsorbent materials of construction, and adequate means of drainage.

24. *Finish.*

The finish of all the equipment should be such as will give maximum wear consistent with ease of cleaning, protection to the workers, and harmony with the surroundings. In most cases smooth hard surfaces are desirable. Glossy surfaces should be avoided.

25. *Color.*

Color is important from the standpoint of æsthetic values and health. Colors which are pleasing and restful to the eye, and which harmonize with the surroundings should be used. Light colors reveal accumulations of dust. Buffs, creams, and flat white are satisfactory for most purposes.

26. *Stability.*

Equipment should be so designed that there is little chance of its upsetting. A large base and a low center of mass are important characteristics of a stable unit.

27. *Minimum Space Requirements.*

Other things being equal, it is desirable to use equipment which occupies the minimum amount of space.

28. *Future Additions and Minor Changes.*

Installations should be made so that additions and minor changes can be made with a minimum cost and minimum inconvenience. Wherever possible, equipment should be chosen and installed with due regard for probable future developments in that or related kinds of equipment. It is sometimes advisable to install conduit and wiring while the building is under construction even if fixtures and the like are not to be supplied at that time.

29. *Flexibility.*

The equipment should be such as is adaptable to use with different subjects and various methods of teaching. It should not interfere with multiple use of the classrooms. When the equipment is portable it should be suitable for use in different parts of the building. It should be adaptable to use with other kinds of instructional equipment.

30. *Special Requirements.*

Designs and installations should be adjusted to meet special demands caused by unusual characteristics of the space to be served. Special legal requirements must be satisfied.

31. *Servicing.*

Only equipment should be installed for which prompt and efficient servicing can be obtained.

32. *Materials.*

The materials used should meet the requirements set up by such organizations as the American Society for Testing Materials, American Society of Mechanical Engineers, American Institute of Electrical Engineers, Radio Manufacturing Association, Electric Power Club, and American Specification Institute.

33. *Supervision of the Services Offered.*

The installation should facilitate control under the organization of the school system.

CHAPTER II

KINDS OF EQUIPMENT NOW AVAILABLE

There are in general two ways in which a school might be equipped for the utilization of high frequency service. Individual sets complete in themselves might be installed in the classrooms, auditorium, gymnasium or wherever desired, or the system might be centralized so that only the loud speakers are located in various places throughout the building. The complete equipment is composed of: (1) the input apparatus—microphone, radio set, or phonograph; (2) the vacuum tube amplifying equipment; and (3) the loud speaker or sound projector.

INDIVIDUAL SETS

When individual radio sets are used the entire equipment including receiver, amplifiers, and speaker is generally in the same room. With this arrangement each set can be operated entirely independently of all others when proper provision has been made for antennae. The provisions for this equipment are exactly the same as those required in a home. In fact, the same kinds of sets are used in the ordinary classrooms. In large rooms like cafeterias, gymnasiums, and auditoriums either especially powerful horns or several speakers are installed. Even when a centralized system is used for the remainder of the building, the auditorium is frequently supplied with an individual set.

Unless the lighting circuit or loops are used for aërials each individual set would require an antenna. Many antennae on a roof would make an unsightly appearance. Some schools use systems of vertical antennae from which lead-ins are taken to the several floors. It is true that individual sets might be used with a system which distributes the radio frequency directly from a single antenna, provided the radio frequency signals have been boosted before they reach the receiver outlets. The latter arrangement is quite expensive and is in reality more nearly a centralized system. A system of this type is described later in this volume as a radio frequency distribution system.

Thus far consideration has been given to space reception only. Programs might be sent over the lighting circuit wires giving the type of service known as "wired radio." Then the properly designed set could be plugged into any electric lighting circuit outlet to receive the particular programs offered by this service. The same kind of service can be obtained where programs are sent over telephone wires, still permitting the telephone wires to be used for the ordinary type of telephone conversation. Provision for service of this kind is under consideration at the present time with the purpose in mind of offering the service to the public. "Wired radio" must not be confused with the arrangement where the wires of the lighting circuit serve as the antenna for space reception.

Sometimes microphones are used with amplifiers and one or more loud speakers to make speech or music audible in large rooms or even outside the building. The individual set might be one in which the input apparatus consists of a phonograph equipped with a magnetic pickup and it may or may not have facilities for radio reception. The combination of phonograph and radio in the same unit is an economy quite popular in homes.

The individual sets to be used in the ordinary classrooms are in all essentials the same as those used for homes. When the sets are to be used in large rooms special equipment is necessary. A discussion of the several items of equipment will be given later.

Centralized Equipment

Distribution of high frequency service is generally accomplished in one of two ways: by using one antenna and distributing untuned radio frequency to individual receiving sets throughout the building; by using one or several central receiving sets and distributing audio frequency to loud speakers located at various places in the building. Radio frequencies are those sent out by a broadcasting station; audio frequencies are those which are detected by the human ear.

Systems Which Distribute Radio Frequencies

When untuned radio frequency is distributed individual sets can be plugged into the system at any outlet and tuned to any program desired, entirely independent of any other sets, provided the capacity of the system is not exceeded. This arrangement is used quite extensively in apartment houses, but its use in schools is limited if it is necessary to have the programs supervised. Its principal application in school buildings is to supply an effective lead-in from the antenna to the receiving set when the two are far from each other. A description of one of these systems follows:

In this system but one ordinary receiving antenna is used, and the radio frequency energy thus received is distributed throughout the building to wall outlets in the individual rooms. From these outlets, the usual antenna, ground and line power connections are made to the radio receiver. A maximum of eighty radio receivers of any type or manufacture can be operated simultaneously from one roof antenna for the reception of programs selected at will, and without interaction or mutual interference. As many more extensions can be accommodated by the use of a second antenna. The undesirable effects of a long or crooked lead-in, such as is necessary to reach the ground floor of a tall building are eliminated. Tests have shown that in some cases stations which otherwise could not be heard at all can be received by means of this system. The list of apparatus required, starting with a suitable antenna equipped with an approved lightning arrester, is as follows:

1. *An Antenna Resistance Unit.*

This unit consists of a capacity unit and a resistance unit suitably mounted inside the first central coupling unit.

2. *A Central Coupling (and Plate Supply) Unit.*

The central coupling assembly consists of a coupling tube, filament supply transformer, radio frequency transformer, condensers, and resistors. The plate supply unit is designed to supply the necessary plate current and voltages for a maximum of 10 extension coupling units and one antenna coupling unit.

3. *Loading Coils.*

Each unit consists of two inductors for mounting in individual boxes or in the extension coupling boxes. One unit is required for approximately every 20 feet of transmission line.

4. *An Extension Coupling Box.*

This unit consists of a coupling tube, filament supply transformer, condensers, and resistors.

5. *A Radio Outlet Unit.*

This unit is of two-gang size, incorporating antenna-ground pin jacks for connection to the receiver, a 110 volt outlet receptacle and switch.

6. *A Line Terminal Unit.*

This resistance and capacity unit is located in space provided in the last extension coupling box on each transmission line.

Systems Which Distribute Audio Frequencies

The centralized systems used most commonly in schools distribute audio frequency obtained from radio receiving sets, microphones, or phonograph pickups. While all of them employ the same general methods they have various trade names such as "Centralized Radio System," "Program Service System," and "Public Address System."

The operation of any system consists essentially of (1) obtaining an incoming signal, (2) amplifying the signal in a usable form, and (3) distributing the signal to operate sound projectors. When signals are received a fluctuating electric current is produced in the system. The fluctuations in the electric current may be initiated electro-mechanically, as in the case of the phonograph pickup; they may be caused by sound vibrations impressed upon a microphone; or they may be the result of high frequency current variations, as in the case of the radio. These current fluctuations enter the amplifier, where their power is greatly increased. When placed upon the circuit for distribution to the loud speaker these fluctuations are of frequencies to which the human ear can respond (audio frequencies). The loud speakers convert the electrical fluctuations into sound and distribute the sound to the audience. Provision is always made for regulating the volume of sound emitted by the loud speakers so that the speech or music can be heard clearly and distinctly by the audience.

Centralized systems may be simple or complex depending upon the kinds of service furnished. At one extreme one would have an ordinary radio receiving set and amplifying unit with several loud speakers or sound projectors located at more or less widely distributed positions. These systems are adaptable to large homes and small school buildings. With the proper use of power amplifiers and loud speakers several of the ordinary sets now on the market will supply programs with ordinary volume (loudness) to 15 stations within a small building. It is not necessary that the input apparatus be a radio receiving set, it might be a phonograph pickup or some form of microphone. Each kind of input apparatus makes possible a different kind of service.

Fixed Central Station.

In the more elaborate centralized equipment, provision is made for all the usual kinds of input: phonograph, microphone, and radio. The associated apparatus is designed so that the change from one kind of service to another can be accomplished by simply operating switches or inserting plugs. The systems are built in units so that the needs of any particular situation can be met easily and installations can be conveniently extended as requirements increase. Provision can be made for one small assembly room with several loud speakers or for almost any number of rooms. The equipment for out-of-doors can be arranged to make speech and music easily audible to 30,000 people.

The large range in volume is another respect in which the flexibility of these outfits is manifest. Although no standards have been established for loudness some idea of relative volume levels can be obtained by comparing the number of loud speakers which can be operated at three different volume levels, without distortion, by one of the standard make amplifiers. If Volume A is desired 33 loud speakers can be operated. This volume level is sufficient for large places like hotel lobbies, entertainment rooms, or large apartments. At Volume B it is possible to operate 66 speakers. The volume will be sufficient for the average room or small apartment. In hotel rooms where it is desirable that the sound be inaudible outside the room, Volume C is used. At this volume level, 198 loud speakers can be operated without any overloading of the output amplifier. Different makes of amplifiers will usually have different power output capacities to handle loud speaker or head set (head phone) loads. Loud speakers vary considerably in the amount of power required to operate them even if they are all of the same general type—dynamic or magnetic. In the above illustration of the power output of an amplifier all the loud speakers have practically the same characteristics and only one amplifier is referred to. Hence, the comparison is significant. The size of the steps between volume levels depends largely upon the opinion of the designer relative to the needs of the consumer. Provision is made in all sets for volume control between any pairs of volume levels. It is quite common to provide for changes in volume level by four distinct steps.

All the more elaborate centralized systems provide for reproduction of music from phonograph records, technically known as phonograph pickup. In some cases the mechanism will operate with records of both the hill-and-dale type like the Edison and the ordinary needle type like the Victor. All the phonograph pickups in common use will operate with the needle type records. These phonograph pickup sets employ electrically driven turntables to rotate the records. Some sets provide double turntables which permit practically continuous music. The reproducing set may also include a fading device by means of which the energy from either reproducer can be placed on the amplifying system. This fading device may act as a volume control also. When fading devices are employed the operator is provided with a head set to monitor on one record while the other is being amplified and broadcast.

In earlier developments of the art of radio, centralized equipment was used primarily in connection with what were commercially known as public address systems. The purpose of these systems was to reproduce, amplify, and project speech or music which had been picked up by one or more transmitters. These transmitters were either regular broadcasting microphones or close-talking telephones. In all the more elaborate modern centralized sets provision is made for the use of broadcasting microphones. Although some manufacturers do not supply the microphones they have designed their equipment so that any standard microphone service can be connected with their systems. The close-talking telephone is a convenient and economical type of transmitter; the person speaking can have his mouth within a very few inches of the mouthpiece while talking. It can be used effectively by the principal of a school to make announcements to classes over the loud speaker circuits.

Several transmitters (microphones) are generally used to pick up the sound produced by large organizations like a symphony orchestra. The energy from these transmitters is fed to a mixer panel where the volume from each of the transmitters is adjusted to the proper value to make the different elements blend so as to produce a satisfactory effect in the reproduction of the sound at the projectors or loud speakers. The blended output is then fed into the amplifying equipment. When speeches are to be picked up from banquet tables the individual transmitters are placed at various places on the tables. These transmitters are connected with a control unit by means of which any particular transmitter can be selected. From this control unit one or more transmitter circuits run to the amplifying equipment either directly or through a mixer panel. On still more elaborate set-ups several mixing panels are employed. Special provisions are generally made to indicate when any particular transmitter or mixing panel is ready for use.

The amplifying equipment for a large centralized system is arranged so that it can be connected directly with the output of any transmitter or group of transmitters, when these transmitters are so located that there is no likelihood of wanting their outputs blended. This situation might exist when the transmitters are located in different rooms in the same building, in different buildings, or out-of-doors.

All the large centralized equipments provide for picking up radio. This is done by the use of radio receiving sets designed for the reception of frequencies within the regular broadcast range. Some sets are now being supplied which will receive short waves. Many different kinds and qualities of sets are used to meet specific requirements of the location as well as to keep the initial cost within the desired range. The makers of elaborate centralized equipment use only such sets as rank high in selectivity, sensitivity, and fidelity. At least one of the outstanding distributors supplies two grades of receivers, one considerably cheaper than the other, but both of them good sets. The cheaper set is a stabilized radio frequency type, while the more expensive one is a double detecting type.

Some centralized receivers are very simple to operate. In one arrangement the receiver can be turned to a given station and the tuning dial locked in position. Then, by means of a time-clock switch the programs can be started and turned off automatically at any designated time.

In some installations the circuits from individual loud speakers or a group of loud speakers are brought to a distributing board. With this arrangement and the proper switching devices it is possible to actuate any desired number of loud speakers, and easy for the operator to connect a test or monitoring loud speaker or head set on any circuit to determine the possible operating characteristic of the speakers or head sets on that circuit. When the volume control is located at the central station it is essential to provide for monitoring. In many installations volume controls are placed on or near the loud speaker. Under these conditions the monitoring is done to determine whether the loud speaker circuit is in proper operating condition. Meters are sometimes used to give a visual indication of the operating conditions. Protective devices such as fuses at the speakers are often included to prevent willful tampering with or accidental damage to any extension from affecting the remainder of the system.

All the large standard centralized outfits have the control apparatus and most, if not all, of the other equipment permanently mounted on substantial racks where ample space has been left for future extensions of the system. In the case of one of the systems which provides for only one program at a time and uses 110 volts AC for power, the space requirements for the entire equipment are two feet by two feet on the floor and seven feet in height. Where storage batteries or motor-generator sets are used additional space must be provided for them, although this additional space need not be in the same room with the control apparatus. Frequently this power equipment is placed in the basement when the control apparatus is on the first floor. If two or more programs are to be distributed over the system simultaneously, an additional central station unit must be furnished for each additional program desired. Some manufacturers speak of installations which will care for two or more simultaneous programs as having two or more channels. The space requirements for even the most elaborate set-ups are small. In tall buildings the control equipment is usually placed in the penthouse. Other favored locations are: the telephone switchboard; in a room adjoining the principal's office; and at the side of the stage in the auditorium.

The metering equipment for different installations varies considerably, but all the better known companies supply the meters essential to an accurate check on the operating conditions of the outfit. When a central station is available furnished with the facilities referred to as common for the standard large centralized systems, it is possible to provide for practically any demands for service that may occur.

The items of equipment mentioned above are more or less common where complete installations have been made. As developments in the art of radio progress it is likely that three additional types of service will be furnished; namely, sound pictures, wired radio, and television. Sound pictures are produced by apparatus which synchronizes the speech and the picture so that the passages spoken by the actors, or the musical accompaniments to the performance will be properly timed with the moving picture. No inherent difficulties exist which might prevent this type of service from being associated with a centralized system. Wired radio refers to transmission of broadcast signals over electric power lines or telephone wires instead of through space as in ordinary radio. If this kind of service is desired the necessary equipment can be made a part of the centralized system since only the radio receiver will be affected. Television when thought of as the transmission of moving pictures by radio, is now in a stage of development that makes it difficult to determine just what provisions must be made to take care of this kind of service. At the present time, space broadcasting of pictures is not practical because the broad bands of frequencies necessary to give distinct pictures interfere with other broadcasting. If the signals were sent over wires this interference would not constitute a serious obstacle.

Portable Central Stations.

The centralized equipment mentioned thus far has been of the fixed type. The systems described have been quite elaborate, but the arrangement is so flexible that it can be suited as well to simple installations. If the installation is not too large and if extension of the service is unlikely, some of the semiportable outfits are quite convenient. If several services like radio, microphone, and phonograph pickup are required the apparatus becomes somewhat bunglesome. There is little reason for moving the amplifier and allied equipment around in any one building. For this reason many portable sets have been installed in fixed positions, such as recesses in walls, or in very small rooms or closets conveniently located. In the Garfield School in Chicago, the central radio service is placed in a space $32'' \times 12'' \times 24''$ which was dug out of the brick wall and faced with a steel door. More space must be allowed if a phonograph pickup and the microphone equipment are to be stored in the same space.

Equipment of portable or semiportable type is particularly convenient for use in auditoriums or assembly halls and where the available space to be served is divided into two or more rooms or halls. The coverage of any system depends upon the amplifying equipment, because any of the good radio sets, microphones, or phonograph pickups will give sufficient signal strength. The amplifier must be related properly to the loud speakers or head sets with which they are to be used.

Manufacturers are placing on the market to-day radio phonograph combinations with power amplifiers and loud speakers designed primarily for use in school auditoriums. The essential features of the apparatus provided in one of these are as follows: The cabinet for the radio receiver, phonograph, and amplifier is of the organ type approximately $4'$ long $\times$ $5'$ high $\times$ $2'$ deep over all. The front chamber of the cabinet affords space for mounting the phonograph turntable, tone arm, magnetic pickup, and needle cups, together with additional space for record albums, and a telephone head set. All the controls are mounted on the panel located within the front chamber. The receiver unit is mounted on a shelf behind the control panel. The two socket power units are mounted on the floor of the cabinet. The receiver is of the superheterodyne type employing automatic volume and sensitivity controls. It has unicontrol tuning. A distortion-indicating meter and resonance-indicating instrument are mounted on the control panel together with a phonograph volume control, "Record-Radio" switch, "Record-Auxiliary Input" switch, and the power switch. Pin jackets are provided for a monitoring head set. The antenna-ground binding posts are mounted near the top of the left side of the cabinet. A floor lamp with suitable shade is mounted at the top of the control panel. In the phonograph equipment the motor, magnetic pickup, tone arm, and the like together with controls are standard phonograph parts. The amplifier employs two UX-250 radiotrons connected in push-pull. The loud speaker consists of four electrodynamic units mounted on a frame in such a manner that two units face 15° to the right and left, respectively, and the other two units face 45° to the right and left, respectively. Each speaker unit is of the twelve-inch cone type. The frame of the whole loud speaker assembly is of steel, and to it is mounted the baffle. A silk screen which may be easily opened for servicing surrounds the front side of the loud speaker. The loud speaker carriage is equipped with four rubber-tired wheels to permit easy moving of the unit in an auditorium. The approximate over-all dimensions of the loud speaker unit are 8′6″ high × 4′6″ wide × 4′6″ deep. The operator's bench is of the organ type. The range of the set is from 550 to 1,500 kilocycles (546 to 200 meters). It is operated from a power supply of 105 to 125 volts at fifty to sixty cycles. This equipment should give ample coverage for an auditorium seating 3,000.

Another type of service which is useful is furnished by systems known commercially as "Announcing Outfits." These outfits consist essentially of a transmitter, an amplifier, and one or more loud speaking telephones. They are intended to transmit orders or information from a person at the transmitter to those within hearing range of the loud speaker or loud speakers. They may be used by an executive to speak to his secretary, between departments where much general information is passed from one to another, or between points where general orders or requests originate and where they are carried out. Such outfits may also be used to announce items of interest to small gatherings and for many other purposes when the listener is not within range of the speaker's voice, and a regular telephone is inconvenient or inadequate. The transmitter may be furnished either in an ornamental mahogany mounting or mounted in the standard desk stand. Three types of announcing outfits can be obtained: the type allowing one-way conversation and providing no means of signaling between the speaker and the listener, or of starting or stopping the outfit except at the power supply switch; the type equipped with a signaling system consisting of a key and a buzzer by means of which the speaker may call the listener (the latter, upon operating a key, starts the system and gives an indication at the transmitter that he is listening); and the type equipped with a key by means of which the speaker may make the system operative from a point remote from the power supply switch, an indication of this being given by a signal lamp. There is, however, no means of signaling to the listener except by talking over the system. With any one of these systems one or more of the various types of loud speakers may be used.

Although centralized systems are of rather recent origin as far as school installations are concerned, enough commercial systems have been tried in other situations to prove that they are thoroughly practical. There is every reason to believe that any reasonable demands which may be made by educators will be met by the manufacturers. Although the radio industry is comparatively new, progress has been so rapid that most of the reliable manufacturers have been forced to keep highly trained experts in their employ. These manufacturers are in a particularly favorable position to deal with any technical problems which may arise.

It is not necessary that the equipment be installed when the building is built; however, this practice is desirable when conduits must be run. At least two ways are open for making installations in old buildings: place the wires along the molding out of sight; use the wires of some other system such as the program bells or the telephone. A recent article by J. C. Duff describes a system installed in the Benjamin Franklin Junior High School, Uniontown, Pennsylvania, whereby one high school principal is making radio programs available. The building was not wired for radio; therefore he utilized the bell circuit for audio frequency distribution. The bell control panel in the principal's office served as the switchboard by which connections were made with any room. He hooked up four rooms to receive the same program. Mr. Duff says:

> The principal by employing a detector plug and a microphone (and a loud speaker will serve as the latter) can speak from the office to any rooms in which loud speakers are connected. . . . The reverse of this hook-up makes the loud speakers in the rooms the microphones. . . . It is a simple matter to install a switch at the set which makes the change or reverse in hook-up instantaneous. By this reversal the principal can speak to the pupils in the classrooms from his office and can hear what is said in reply by merely throwing the switch.[1]

[1] Duff, J. C. "Radio as a Means to Instruction." *School Executives Magazine*, Vol. 43, No. 5, pp. 210-11, January 1929.

While speaking of using the phonograph pickup Mr. Duff says, "By a combination of the electrical pickup and a recording device, records of interesting radio events can be made and reproduced when desired." He plans to install an attachment that will permit the use of telephones in connection with the radio amplification circuit. Another system which might be used in old buildings is described as Installation Number 4 under suggested installations, Appendix A.

When several schools of a system are equipped for radio it is a distinct advantage to tie the services together so that local broadcasting can be done, particularly between schools of the same grade level—several high schools, for instance. Because of the cost of equipment and the difficulty of obtaining broadcasting permits when radio frequencies are used, it seems advisable to do the local broadcasting over wires and to use audio frequencies. Some engineers are of the opinion that the cost involved in transmitting programs over wires would be prohibitive in many communities unless arrangements could be made with the telephone company for special toll rates. The use of the wires of the city fire alarm system offers another possibility. An experiment with this arrangement was conducted in New York City in the summer of 1929 in connection with the transmission of programs to the city parks. Local conditions will determine what particular arrangement can be used most economically.

Some suggested radio installations for schools are given in Appendix A.

CHAPTER III

INDIVIDUAL ITEMS OF EQUIPMENT OF AN AUDIO FREQUENCY SYSTEM

This chapter deals with each of the major items of equipment which go into the make-up of a complete audio frequency distribution system. Consideration is given to the characteristics of each part as a unit, to the relation of each part to the whole system, and to the external conditions affecting the unit. The treatment is made with the audio frequency distribution systems as the basis because the radio frequency distribution systems which are designed for use with independent receiving sets in tall buildings have only limited value in the ordinary school buildings. The use which can be made of some features of the radio distribution system are considered in this chapter under "Antenna and Lead-In Equipment." Individual receiving sets are not treated as such because the discussions given here cover all the important features of these sets as well.

In order to follow a logical sequence each unit is considered in the order of encounter experienced if a signal is traced back to its original source from the point where the listener obtains direct contact with the set. Although this is the reverse order in the sense of signal transmission it is the normal order in which the casual observer should think of the system when considering the service to be rendered.

LOUD SPEAKERS AND SOUND PROJECTION

The function of the loud speaker is to convert electrical energy into sound energy. Loud speakers are in reality special types of loud speaking telephones. Four outstanding types of loud speakers are on the market to-day. They are known in the trade as (1) magnetic type, (2) dynamic type, (3) induction type, and (4) condenser type. Each of these types of speakers has certain advantages. Until within the past two years the magnetic loud speakers were used almost exclusively. The demand for the dynamic speaker has grown tremendously within the past year because comparatively small units which will produce low notes and a considerable volume of sound are desired. The ideal sound radiator has been defined as a plane of infinite rigidity without mass, freely suspended in the air without mechanical friction, tension, or stress. Such a diaphragm would have perfect damping, no natural period, no flexural, reflected, or standing waves. The condenser type of speaker is highly efficient in converting electrical energy into sound energy, and it approaches the theoretically ideal diaphragm more nearly than any other diaphragm known to science at the present time. It seems quite probable that the condenser type of loud speaker will be particularly well suited for school installations if future developments result in construction characteristics similar to those recently invented by Colvin Kyle. The thinness of this loud speaker (approximately one-eighth of an inch) makes it adaptable to many unique designs and makes the space requirements for installations small, at least where depth is concerned. In the present stage of development of the art of sound reproduction only the magnetic (moving iron or armature) and the dynamic (moving coil) types of loud speakers are of practical importance for school installations.

Moving Iron Type Loud Speakers (Magnetic).

The magnetic loud speakers differ from the electrodynamic or electromagnetic (usually referred to as dynamic) types: in the former a moving iron or balanced armature type of drive is employed to actuate the diaphragm; in the latter a moving coil is used for that purpose. The magnetic loud speaker is in reality an oversized telephone unit. In fact, when loud speakers were first placed on the market many amateurs made their own by attaching a horn to the receivers of the familiar headphone set. It is true that this kind of homemade speaker did not produce much volume.

Horn Type Magnetic Loud Speakers.

The horn type loud speaker really consists of two units, the receiver and the horn. Some receivers have a metal diaphragm which vibrates before the pole pieces of a permanent magnet like a very powerful telephone receiver. In other receivers the diaphragm is connected by means of a system of levers to an armature which vibrates between the pole pieces of the magnet.

In neither of these types is the diaphragm attached directly to the horn. Horns used on the better modern loud speakers are much larger and much more scientifically constructed than were those used on the older makes of speakers. In papers by Goldsmith and Minton [1] and in others dealing with the performance and theory of loud speaker horns, the following conditions were considered important: (1) the opening of the horn should be reasonably large; (2) the cross section should increase slowly and logarithmically; and (3) the neck of the horn must be rigid. The horn must be of some nonresonant material, such as papier mâché or cement, to prevent resonance. The lower the notes to be produced the longer the horn must be. Good horns have air columns up to 21 feet. When space is a consideration, horns are used in which the throat is wound around or under the bell. The magnetic horn type loud speakers are good for voice reproduction. The response is sharp and distinct because of the small inertia of the moving parts. Horns are extremely directional in their output, and for this reason can be used advantageously to supply restricted areas and to aid in correcting acoustical faults in large rooms.

Cone Type Magnetic Loud Speakers.

In the cone type loud speakers the cone itself is the diaphraghm which sets the surrounding air into motion, thus producing the sound waves which are detected by the human ear. Cone type loud speakers may be grouped into two classes: closed type, having two shallow cones with their bases together; open type with a single light cone which resembles a bell. The mechanism common to most cone speakers is like that of a Baldwin telephone. A small rod is connected to an armature which vibrates in step with the current passing through the windings around the pole pieces of a permanent magnet, between which the armature is located. The other end of the rod is connected to the apex of a paper or cloth cone. The cone, which may be loosely connected around the periphery, is said to act like a rigid piston

[1] Goldsmith, A. N. and Minton, J. P. "The Performance and Theory of Loud Speaker Horns." *Proceedings, Institute of Radio Engineers*, Vol. 12, (August 1924), No. 4, pp. 445-46.

for low frequencies. It responds to the high frequencies like a wave conductor. When the cone is constructed of paper it has practically no frequencies of its own and it brings out the low register of the orchestra. According to Rice and Kellogg [2] no loud speakers respond equally to all frequencies, all have some resonance which accentuates some notes and represses others. These authors consider paper cones better than horns. Because of the relatively large inertia of the moving parts of the cone diaphragms there is some loss in the sharpness and distinctness of reproduction of speech. Cone loud speakers are very good for music reproduction.

Moving Coil Type Loud Speakers (Dynamic)

Loud speakers which utilize a moving coil to drive the diaphragm are known commercially as electromagnetic, or electrodynamic, or, even more commonly, as dynamic. The operation of the moving coil drive is based upon the principle that if a current-carrying conductor is placed in a magnetic field there will be developed mechanical forces between the conductor and the magnet. More specifically, if a wire loop is suspended between the poles of a fixed magnet it will move when a current is passed through it. When the magnetic field strength produced by the fixed magnet is maintained constant, the direction and amplitude of motion of the coil depends upon the direction and strength of the current. In a loud speaker the wire loop is a coil of many turns, the current passing through it is the alternating audio frequency signal current, and the fixed magnet is an electromagnet supplied with direct current. The operation consists of movements of the coil corresponding in frequency and amplitude with the signal current, these movements being transmitted to the cone or other diaphragm to which the coil is attached, and the diaphragm in turn radiating the sound.

As in the case of the moving iron (magnetic) loud speakers there are two types of moving coil (dynamic) loud speakers; namely, the cone type and the horn type. No separate discussion of the horn and cone types of loud speakers is given here because the distinctions between the two types of speakers are the same whether they employ the moving coil drive (dynamic)

[2] Rice, C. W. and Kellogg, E. W. "Notes on the Development of a New Type Loud Speaker." *Journal of the American Institute of Electrical Engineers*, Vol. 44, September 1925, pp. 982-91.

or the moving iron drive (magnetic). Various horn type dynamic speakers have been in use for many years while the first cone type dynamic speaker was placed on the market in 1925. Probably the most highly developed form of moving coil drive is used in the large horn type speakers for movietone and vitaphone installations. For school use the horn type speaker is not as readily adaptable as the cone type because of the size of the horns required for good reproduction. There are some places, however, like the auditorium where space for large horns might be provided without much trouble. Horn type speakers with horns six or more feet in length are equally as good as cone speakers with respect to the quality of the tone reproduced. The following data for three horns are given to show the sizes of horns needed to produce satisfactory tones down to certain frequencies: (1) Length of air column 6 feet; diameter of mouth of bell 2'6"; frequency cutoff point 115 cycles (near the lower limit of the average male speaking voice). (2) Length of sound passage 14 feet; opening in bell 62" wide and 46" high, frequency cutoff point 57 cycles (near A in the third octave below middle C which has a frequency of 256), which is below the range of the human voice. (3) Length of sound passage 21 feet; mouth opening 7' square, cutoff point 36 cycles (near the end of the third octave below middle C, practically the lower limit of the musical scale). These horns may be used with either the moving coil (dynamic) or the moving iron (magnet) drive receiver.

In both magnetic and dynamic types of loud speakers precautions must be taken to prevent the air in front of the diaphragm from escaping around the edges. This is necessary in order to avoid the forward thrust of the diaphragm and amounts to enabling the diaphragm to get a grip on the air. The action which takes place where no provision is made to prevent the air from escaping around the edges of the diaphragm can be explained as follows. Upon the forward thrust of the diaphragm the air pressure immediately in front of it is increased, while the pressure immediately in the rear is decreased. The compressed air in front tends to slip around the edges of the diaphragm into the rarefied region in the rear, with the result that the pressure becomes immediately equalized since the pressure differences have disappeared. No sound results because sound consists of pressure differences propagated through the air as waves. Some method must be employed which will increase the distance the compression or rarefaction must travel before it will reach a place where an opposite pressure condition exists. This is done by increasing the air path from the front to the rear of the speaker. In the case of the horn type loud speaker this spilling effect is prevented by the horn itself. Baffles are used for the same purpose with the cone type speakers. A baffle may be in the form of a flat board, a box, a widely flaring cone, or a pyramid. The use of baffles is necessary with any type of single cone speaker, but its importance is more marked in the case of the dynamic speaker because so much emphasis is placed on the low tones. A six-inch cone without a baffle cannot radiate effectively below 550 cycles which is approximately an octave above middle C on the piano. At high frequencies (high tones) where the waves are short compared with the cone diameter, a baffle is unnecessary, but at low frequencies (low tones) with their consequent long sound waves the path from front to rear of the cone must be made correspondingly long. For 60 cycles, the diameter of a flat baffle must be about 4 feet. Some of the troubles experienced with the single cone speaker are largely overcome in those speakers having double cones with their bases together because the two cones operate in unison, that is, compressions start from the front and back of the cone at the same time.

Baffles were discussed at this point because reference is made to them in the following list of advantages and disadvantages of the dynamic speakers.

Advantages of the Properly Constructed Moving Coil (Dynamic) Loud Speaker.

1. Both low and high frequencies can be reproduced if proper baffles are provided.

2. The problem of getting sufficient power into the speaker over the whole frequency range is simplified because the impedance (apparent resistance to an alternating current) does not change greatly with the frequency.

3. Great volume can be obtained when the speaker is fed from a sufficiently large power amplifier. A dynamic speaker has a high load capacity without serious distortion. This means that

the speaker can handle a large amount of power without any serious changes taking place in the waves as they pass through it. It is extremely important that distortion be kept at a minimum if the sound output from the speaker is to be like the sound impressed upon the system.

4. Some cone dynamic speakers occupy comparatively small space, especially when the enclosing case is used as the baffle.

Disadvantages of the Moving Coil (Dynamic) Loud Speaker.

1. The expense involved in manufacture is several times as great for a good moving coil speaker as it is for a good moving iron speaker.

2. A good dynamic speaker requires great precision in manufacture. For high efficiency the moving coil must as completely as possible fill the air gap between the pole pieces without touching their sides. This clearance is sometimes as small as 0.005 of an inch. Poor quality may result from hasty manufacture for a price-competitive market.

3. For all dynamic speakers now on the market an extra source of power is required for field excitation. This power requirement for different speakers ranges from about 3 to 25 watts. Because of the difficulty of making speakers with extremely small clearance between the moving coil and the pole pieces, manufacturers prefer to use safer clearance and larger field currents. If the power supply is taken from an alternating current source, provision must be made to eliminate the alternating current hum. This can be accomplished by connecting a condenser, about 2,000 microfarads, across the field coil.

4. Low sensitivity will result if there is carelessness in manufacture or design, and if a strong field is not supplied. The result would be that the amplifier supply power to the speaker would be overloaded before sufficient output volume would be obtained from the speaker.

5. The speakers are quite heavy—10 to 30 pounds—but this weight is not objectionable if the speakers are intended for permanent mounting in protected places.

6. High power amplifiers must be employed to get full benefit of the load capacity of a dynamic speaker. Extremely high volume levels are of no value except in large places like auditoriums or halls.

7. The position of the listener with respect to the loud speaker may have a decided effect upon the quality of the reproduction heard. This is due to the fact that the good dynamic speaker can reproduce very high frequencies which are strongly directive.

The list of advantages and disadvantages given above has special reference to the moving coil loud speakers. The following are characteristics of speakers which must be carefully considered but which are not necessarily associated with any particular type of speaker.

Resonance Troubles.

Paper cone loud speakers have a tendency to produce an unpleasant shrillness in the reproduction because of cone resonance at high frequencies. To eliminate this fault means are sometimes employed which result in cutting off much of the high frequency range (high musical notes) with a decidedly bad effect upon the quality of reproduction. The cutting off of high frequencies takes away crispness and distinctness, and removes sibilants from speech.

No loud speaker responds equally to all frequencies. All of them have some resonance which accentuates some notes and represses others. As a rule there is less difficulty with paper cones than there is with horns. Horns must be made of non-resonant material or they will resonate notes depending upon their length.

Because of the apparent limitations of paper cones, some manufacturers have introduced recently an impregnated cloth diaphragm. A unique form of diaphragm material known as "burtex" is made of a special fabric pressed to the desired shape and then impregnated with a waterproof compound. This diaphragm is said to hold its shape indefinitely and to be non-resonant. It is a one-piece diaphragm, even the edge support is made in the form of an extension of the cone while the voice coils of the dynamic speaker may be included in the single piece by using a properly formed apex.

Since horns are all relatively long the resonant tones produced by them will be of low frequency. If tones below the resonance frequencies are not needed more liberty can be taken in matters of materials of construction used. Data for three horns are given below to show what kinds of materials are used in horns with different cut-off points, the lowest frequencies that will be emitted with satisfactory quality: (1) Cut-off point 115 cycles, air column 6 feet, the throat portion is constructed in two sections and made of cast aluminum, the bell portion is made of fibre. (2) Cut-off point 57 cycles, air column 14 feet, the throat is made of cast iron, the folded body and the bell portion are of wood. (3) Cut-off point 36 cycles, air column 21 feet, the throat is made of cast iron, body and bell portions are of wood.

While the baffle can do much good in its operation it may also prove very troublesome. The box baffle has the disadvantage that the enclosure of the sides forms a cavity behind the cone in which resonance disturbances are set up at low frequencies. This resonance gives to the speaker a barrel tone, or booming sound, as it is commonly called. The effect is particularly bad if the box is deep or partially closed at the rear. Such speakers should not be set close to a wall unless the sides are freely vented and even then bad resonance may occur. There should be free circulation of the air both in front of and behind the speaker. Free circulation of the air behind the mechanism eliminates troublesome nasal sounds. The baffle itself might resonate at certain low frequencies. The best way to overcome this trouble is to use only nonresonant materials of construction. The baffle should be thick enough that it will not vibrate readily. Thin wood and loose pieces should not be used.

Loud Speaker Rattle.

It is always necessary to know at what input energy level a loud speaker will operate without producing a sound which resembles paper rattle. The manufacturer should state the maximum alternating current voltage that the loud speaker will stand without rattle. These voltages should be given for a sufficient number of frequencies to reveal the operation throughout the frequency range. Some engineers prefer to express this same characteristic in terms of audio frequency power in watts.

Within the high frequency range near 5,000 cycles, tube overloading resembles a paper rattle, due to generation of harmonies and combination tones. The trouble can be relieved by making the cut-off so low that the quality of reproduction of the higher frequencies is interfered with. Slight warping or other deformation of the cone of a loud speaker tends to increase the paper rattle to a marked degree. Specially corrugated cones are sometimes used to reduce paper rattle.

The Coupling of the Loud Speaker to Its Associated Amplifiers.

The loud speaker must be correctly coupled with the amplifier which feeds the energy to it. In order to match the speaker and the amplifier properly the impedance of the last tubes and the speaker must be known. With the ordinary moving iron (magnetic) speaker which has impedance of several thousand ohms the coupling is quite simple because the impedance of the last amplifier tubes is high also. The magnetic speaker may be worked directly out of the output tube of the amplifier, or with the use of a capacity-choke to keep direct current out of the speaker windings. Where much power is used and especially in the case of moving coil (dynamic) speakers, the coupling is generally made through a transformer so designed that the impedance of the power tube and the loud speaker will be matched. The impedance of the moving coil in the dynamic speakers is only about five to fifteen ohms while that of the amplifier tubes with which they work is several thousand ohms. Consequently, the transformer is necessary to stop the impedance of the moving coil up to a value comparable with that of the tube. The desirable characteristics of this type of coupling unit are given later under "Audio Frequency Transformers." It is also essential that the loud speaker and its supplying equipment be properly matched with respect to audio frequency range.

Fidelity.

Fidelity is a term which is applied to those charactersitics of reproducing instruments which indicate the degree of faithfulness with which sounds are reproduced. Volume output and fidelity are the two characteristics of loud speakers which are most commonly used as bases for comparing different loud speakers. When certain frequencies are suppressed and others are accentuated to a very marked degree, the fidelity of the reproduction is seriously affected. Narrow range, improperly constructed diaphragms, inadequate baffling, lack of match between the loud speaker and its associated amplifier, improper balance between low frequency and high frequency outputs, poorly constructed horns, and lack of allowance for external influences upon the speaker all contribute to poor fidelity. One of the most common causes of poor reproduction in a good speaker is the tendency to try to obtain more volume from the unit than that for which it has been designed. The distortion which results is caused by the overloading of the power amplifier. Fidelity is judged almost entirely on a personal basis. It is a common practice in making tests to place the loud speakers where they cannot be seen by the judges and then have the latter render their decisions as to the relative merits of the units under consideration. These tests are conducted with the speakers in surroundings like those in which they are to be used.

Characteristics of Sound Which Influence the Interpretation of Loud Speaker Output.

In order to have a real appreciation of the results produced by a loud speaker it is necessary to recall a few of the characteristics of sound which so greatly influence sound reproduction and also some of the peculiar interpretations which the listener places upon the sound produced. Physically, sound is a wave motion consisting of compressions and rarefactions of the medium in which it travels. These sound waves enter the ear as a succession of minute changes in air pressure. The speed with which these disturbances travel depends upon the kind of medium in which they travel and upon the temperature, density, and elasticity of the medium. In dry air at 32° F. the speed of sound is about 1,100 feet per second. Unless restricted in some way, sound will travel from the source in concentric circles. The energy in the disturbance varies inversely as the square of the distance from the source. Consequently, the energy will be one-fourth as great when the distance from the source is doubled if all other conditions remain the same. In the air, sound waves can be reflected, absorbed, and refracted. Like other wave disturbances they will interfere with and reinforce each other. If sound waves of a certain frequency strike an object which has a natural period of this frequency the object will vibrate (resonate) with the result that this tone will be reinforced. Resonance will also take place in an air space, provided the dimensions of this space bear the proper relation to the frequency of the entering sound wave.

Many of the reinforcement and interference effects encountered in places where loud speakers are involved are associated with reflection. The reflected waves result from many reflections producing a prolonged ringing (reëcho) effect known as reverberation or they may be due to reflection from a single surface giving an ordinary echo. Both of these effects may prove either troublesome or beneficial. Reverberation is necessary to give life to a sound, but too much reverberation results in the prolongation of each tone emitted to such a degree that the effect is unpleasant. Acoustical difficulties resulting from single reflections are most serious when the echoes return to the emitting source in time to interfere with the succeeding tones emitted. Sometimes the reflected and the on-coming waves meet in such a way that standing waves are produced with the result that at certain places there will be no sound at all while halfway between these places the sound will be reinforced. Troubles due to reflection are generally corrected by providing for more absorption of the sound waves. The ability to absorb sound energy depends upon the character of the absorbing material and also upon the sound frequency to be absorbed. Small absorption at any frequency results in an increase in the intensity at that frequency while the opposite is true of high absorption. It is immediately apparent that the material used in the construction and decoration of a room has a decided effect upon the character of the sound emitted in that room. Wente [3] favors wood paneling over hair felt or cloth hangings for the absorbers because hair felt absorbs most in the high frequencies while the wood absorbs more readily in the low frequencies. Wente was influenced in his decision by the work of Crandall and MacKenzie [4] which indicated that 50 per cent of speech energy is below frequencies of 500 cycles per second while 20 per cent is below 200 cycles per second. This shows that half of the speech energy is in frequencies corresponding to tones which are lower than one octave above the speaking voice of the average woman. On the other hand, as far as intelligibility is concerned, speech is almost perfect if all frequencies in the above limits are elimi-

[3] Wente, E. C. "The Effect of the Acoustics of an Auditorium on the Interpretation of Speech." *The American Architect*, August 20, 1928, Vol. CXXXIV, No. 2551.

[4] Crandall, I. B. and MacKenzie, Donald. "Energy Distribution of Speech." *Physical Review*, March 1922, Vol. XIX, p. 221.

nated. Morecroft, Pinto and Curry [5] point out that intelligibility of speech is nearly perfect if all frequencies below 1,000 are eliminated, although practically all the energy of the voice is below 1,000. Moreover, the ear is less sensitive to higher frequencies. These are extremely important considerations in loud speaker design because of the danger of overemphasizing the low frequencies.

Referring to loud speaker characteristics Wolff [6] calls attention to four outstanding points to be noted in determining the fidelity of a loud speaker: low frequency cut-off; high frequency cut-off; smoothness of response between the cut-offs; the balance between the low and high frequencies. If low frequencies are cut off the reproduction loses fullness and body while if the high frequencies are not reproduced there is a loss in crispness and distinctness. In order to have the proper relation between the low and the high frequencies the output of the speaker should be such that above and below 1,000 cycles the tonal frequency response will about balance when the response curve is plotted on a logarithmic or musical frequency scale. When a loud speaker has a narrow frequency range like 400 to 3,000 cycles the tones produced are "metallic." This metallic quality is largely removed and the tones are richer if the frequency range is increased to 200 to 4,000 cycles. If certain frequencies near ends of the range are much stronger than the others the untrained listener will judge the range to be larger than it really is.

The following frequency ranges are given to indicate the limits within which a loud speaker must be able to operate if it is to reproduce certain kinds of music and speech. The frequency of the average male voice is about 128 cycles per second, while that of the female voice is about 256. Frequencies as high as 8,000 or 9,000 cycles exist in various speech sounds. The range from 25 to 4,000 cycles covers practically all of the tones (not including overtones) produced by the organ and piano and all of the instruments of the orchestra. Harmonies and overtones are produced with frequencies of 8,000 and above. Frequencies above 20,000 cycles are not perceived as sound. The upper frequency limit for hearing decreases with the age of the listener.

[5] Morecroft, John H., Pinto, A. and Curry, W. A. *Principles of Radio Communication*, p. 755, (2d ed.). John Wiley and Sons, Inc., 1927.

[6] Wolff, Irving. "Some Measurements and Loud Speaker Characteristics." *Proceedings, Institute of Radio Engineers*, December 1928, Vol. 16, No. 12, p. 1732.

A good summary of the pressure and frequency characteristics of sound in relation to its effect upon the ear is represented diagrammatically in Figures 1 and 2 which were taken from an article by Steinberg.[7] In both figures the scale of abscissas (the horizontal scale) is frequencies in cycles per second and the ordinate (the vertical scale) is the pressure in dynes. Logarithmic scales are used on both ordinates because of the logarithmic relationship which exists between our mental responses and the physical stimuli producing these characteristics —between pitch and frequency, and between loudness and pressure. The scale on the right of each figure is an arbitrary loud-

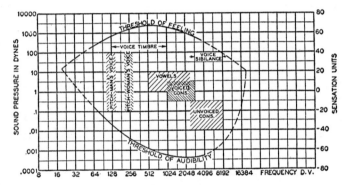

Fɪɢ. 1. Any sound that can be heard lies within the field outlined here· Areas covered by the most prominent speech sounds are indicated.

ness scale, the units of which, called sensation units, are defined as twenty times the logarithm of the pressure. These sensation units are sometimes called decibels and are abbreviated *db*. The boundary marked "Threshold of Audibility" indicates low limit of the pressures which are necessary for each frequency in order that that particular sound may be heard. This curve indicates that as the frequencies increase (pitch rises) the pressure necessary for audibility decreases. The upper boundary marked "Threshold of Feeling" indicates the pressures at which feeling begins for each frequency (pitch). Excessive pressures above this boundary cause actual pain.

In addition to the constants given in the preceding paragraph, Figure 1 furnishes the following approximate numerical values.

[7] Steinberg, John C. "Fundamentals of Speech, Hearing and Music." *Bell Laboratories Record*, November 1928.

Voice timbre is obtained from frequencies 128 to 1,024 cycles and voice sibilance is produced in the frequencies 2,900 to 8,000 cycles. The frequencies for vowel sounds extend from 512 to 2,200 cycles, those for voiced consonants from 1,024 to 2,900 cycles, and those for unvoiced consonants, 2,200 to 8,192 cycles. This figure indicates that the sound pressure for pitches corresponding to the speaking voice of either a man or a woman ranges from 0.1 to 100 dynes per square centimeter, for vowels from 1 to 10 dynes; for voiced consonants from approximately 0.35 to 1 dyne, and for unvoiced consonants from 0.01 to 0.35 dyne. These values indicate that a reproducer with a narrow

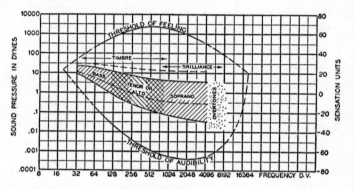

Fig. 2.   Constant loudness lines are not quite horizontal but slope down with increasing frequency as shown.

range of frequencies properly placed might adequately serve speech where quality is not important and where some degree of distinctness can be sacrificed. This situation might exist in a school installation if the outfit is to be used primarily for announcement purposes, or where the loud speaker is used as a microphone to listen in on classes. The latter arrangement is theoretically possible and has been used with some degree of success in amateur installations. It is doubtful whether any sacrifices should be made which materially decrease the naturalness of the reproduction.

Figure 2 shows contour lines (upper and lower boundaries of the shaded areas) of equal loudness for the frequency range from 32 to 4,000 cycles produced by musical instruments. If all frequencies produced equal loudness with the same sound pressure these contour lines would be horizontal. In reality, the notes of the lower registers have greater sound pressures than those of the higher. The range of pressures (indicated as the vertical distance between lower and upper contour lines) for the low notes is narrower than for the high notes. The contour line indicates that music played softly will cover a greater pressure than loud music. The timbre of the sound produced by musical instruments is indicated in this figure as coming from the frequency range of 30 to 1,000 cycles, while the brilliants are produced in the frequency range of 1,300 to 8,000 cycles. It is therefore evident that speakers with large frequency ranges must be employed in schools where good reproduction of music is desired. That is one of the most important reasons for using the moving coil (electrodynamic) speaker in the auditorium, music rooms, and other rooms where it is desired to make a critical study of the music reproduced.

Lower pitched tones in a sound tend to deafen the listener to higher tones, this deafening or masking effect increases as the sound pressure increases. For this reason, the most faithful reproduction will be obtained when the sounds are reproduced with about the same loudness as the original.

In summarizing the results obtained by a large number of investigators Morecroft, Pinto and Curry [8] point out the following facts regarding the nature of speech:

1. Vowel sounds in general are low frequency, they are easy to amplify and transmit. Consonants are very weak.
2. Frequencies encountered in human speech range from 100 to 6,000 complete vibrations.
3. Energy in speech is mostly in frequencies below 500, but quality and intelligibility are produced by frequencies higher than 500.
4. The average power output of the normal voice is 75 ergs per second or 7.5 microwatts.
5. The human ear can detect sounds at frequencies of about 1,000 cycles per second if the pressure of sound wave is as low as .001 dyne/cm^2 (weight of a human hair having a length 1/3 the diameter). If the pressure exceeds 1,000 dynes/cm^2 at this frequency the ear is practically paralyzed and the sensation is that of feeling.
6. The ratio of the peak power of the human voice (manifest in accented syllables) to average may be 200 to 1; thus the average human voice of ten microwatts shows peaks of 2,000 microwatts.

[8] Morecroft, Pinto and Curry, *op. cit.*, pp. 753-54.

External Conditions Affecting the Loud Speaker.

The functioning of a loud speaker must always be thought of in connection with the surroundings in which the unit is being used. The position of the speaker in the room is extremely important. Many instances of poor reproduction have been remedied by a simple shift of the loud speaker to another part of the room or to an adjacent room. Where loud speakers are used for sound reproduction they should be shielded and should project the sound away from the microphone. This precaution is particularly important when horns are used as the projectors. Many engineers try to allow several feet, preferably as much as ten feet between the position of the microphone and the bell of the horn of a horn type speaker. If the microphone and the reproducer are in the same room the best results are obtained by using the horn type speakers. If the speaker and microphone are not in the same room then better quality can be obtained with smaller equipment by using other than the horn type. The horn type speaker is particularly well adapted to directing sound and correcting echoes and reverberations. For radio and record reproduction it is frequently desirable to have the sound well diffused over the area to be served. Cone type speakers are convenient for this purpose.

All loud speakers are directive, some of them very much so. Horn type speakers are the most directive, the open cone type next, and the closed cone type the least directive. Most speakers radiate more sound forward from the radiating surface, particularly at high frequencies. This means that there will be a greater high frequency response directly in front of the speaker. The ratio of the high frequency response to the low frequency response is affected by the absorption characteristics of the place in which the speaker is located. When the absorption for any frequency is small most of the sound entering the ear will have been reflected many times and will not be coming directly from the speaker. On the other hand, if the absorption is great the larger part of the sound will be emitted from the speaker in the direction in which the speaker is pointed. Therefore, the relative energy densities for different frequencies at a position directly in front of the position will remain practically the same if the speaker is in a room having high absorption for all frequencies, or out-of-doors. However, if the room has small absorption the energy density ratios will be very much different from those emitted by the loud speaker. The low tones drop off when the speaker is placed out-of-doors. Actually the situation is still more complicated in rooms because the absorption is not uniform at all frequencies. Small absorption at any frequency leads to an increase in intensity at that frequency; the opposite is true for high absorption. The ordinary classroom and its equipment are constructed largely of wood, thus making the absorption of sound relatively small. In a home there are cloth hangings, rugs, and other furnishings which absorb sound readily. Consequently the sound produced in the former will have the high frequency tones more influenced by reflection. There are some loud speakers on the market that can be changed from normal output to accentuation of the low frequency by simply operating one switch which throws the condenser capacity across the speaker input.

Under certain conditions the air in the room may resonate to certain frequencies. This resonance might be excited if the loud speaker were closely coupled to the air in the room. Resonance effects may be good or bad depending upon what is reinforced and what is destroyed. Sometimes placing a speaker in the corner of a room increases the quality of reproduction, especially of the low notes. Here the space between the speaker and the walls acts as a resonance chamber for vibrations from the rear side of the speaker diaphragm of cone type speakers.

When a speaker is to be located account must be taken of all the conditions discussed above; namely, room absorption and reflection characteristics, resonance in the room, and the position of the listener with respect to the loud speaker. In order to overcome the directive effect of speakers they should be pointed so as to cover as large a portion of the audience as possible. When several speakers are placed in the same room they should be located so that sound from all speakers will reach any given part of the room at practically the same time. Many engineers meet this requirement by placing the speakers in clusters. The individual speakers in the cluster are pointed in different directions so that the projected sound will cover the entire audience.

The two most favored places for the location of the loud speakers in school auditoriums are: (1) in the center of the space immediately above the stage opening; (2) in the spaces to the sides of the stage opening and well out of reach of the pupils. The second arrangement is considered bad by some because of the danger of not getting the sound so distributed that reproduction from one speaker will correspond with that from the other. Some engineers will not consider placing loud speaker units more than ten feet apart in the same general part of the room. In very large auditoriums it is sometimes necessary to put several groups of speakers in widely separated parts of the room, but when this is done the engineer strives to make the arrangement such that at any particular place in the audience the sound seems to come from a single source. When microphones are used with loud speakers care must be taken to prevent directing the sound from the loud speaker on the microphone.

The general practice for locating speakers in the classrooms is to place them either on the front wall or on the side wall adjacent to the corridor and usually at a level just above the blackboard. There are advantages and disadvantages in both of these locations. The locations will be evaluated in terms of the following criteria for the location of loud speakers:

1. The reproductions should come to the listener from the reproducing equipment in such a direction as produces the most natural and comfortable effect. For classroom work this condition is best met when the sound radiator is on a level with the ear and in front of the listener.

2. There should be maximum coverage at the best quality of reproduction. This is particularly important for speakers which are highly directive.

3. There should be maximum protection from willful or accidental injury.

4. There should be proper relation to the acoustic properties of the room.

5. The sound conducted into other rooms should be a minimum (unless two rooms are to be served by the same loud speaker).

6. Construction difficulties should be minimized. This is especially important for flush wall-mounted speakers.

7. Interference with other necessary equipment should be minimized.

8. The speaker should be convenient to operate and convenient to service.

Both the side wall and front wall locations are satisfactory with respect to protection from injury, and convenience of operation especially when the controls are placed low enough to be reached easily.   When one loud speaker is used the front wall location will give the better coverage.   If two speakers are used the side wall location is better, primarily because it is easier to overcome the ordinary acoustic difficulties in a room when the sound is projected across the shorter axis.   The side wall location is also better from the standpoint of sound conducted into other rooms.   When a loud speaker is placed on the front wall it may be in the way of the picture screen.   This objection does not hold when the speaker is mounted flush with the wall. When flush type speakers are used another difficulty arises because of the thickness of the ordinary partition walls.   When these walls are not bearing walls the usual thickness is about six inches and the ordinary magnetic loud speakers of different makes require a depth of from four to twelve inches to clear the outfit.   Even at the maximum depth much of the sound radiated from the rear of the speaker will be heard in the next room unless special sound insulators are placed behind the speaker.   It is possible, however, to use one loud speaker for two adjoining rooms if the front of the loud speaker opens into one room and the rear into the other room.   This arrangement is perfectly feasible, especially if the closed cone type of speaker is used as both sides of this speaker radiate the sound quite strongly.   Some homes have been equipped with open cone type speakers mounted in the partition walls to serve two adjoining rooms.   Adequate provisions were made for cutting off the sound from either room.   This type of installation is not common in schools, but it has possibilities if the cost of the installation must be kept at a minimum.

When a speaker is located above the blackboard or at any other corresponding level the sound will be directed over the heads of the children unless the speaker is tilted.   In some speakers the mechanism is such that tilting the unit interferes with its operation.

The author recommends locating the loud speaker in the corner of the room between the door into the corridor and the front wall.   In this location the speaker could be placed at any height desired, the baffle could be built to meet any reasonable requirements, adjustments of the equipment could be made without causing any construction difficulties, servicing could be done conveniently, the air space between the speaker and the wall could be used as a resonance chamber if desired, the speaker would be near the position where the conduits for other electric wiring terminate, it would not be necessary to run a conduit in the thin partition walls, the equipment could be so enclosed and locked that it would not be subject to injury, the speaker would direct the sound along a diagonal of the room and therefore give maximum coverage. It would be easier to prevent sound from being conducted into the adjoining room from this location than from a point on the front wall, there would be no serious interference with other necessary equipment, and the outfit would be in a convenient position for operation. This location would not be suitable if two rooms were to be served by the same loud speaker. When the engineers installed the radio equipment in the Tremont School at Cleveland they located the loud speakers in a front corner of the room.

Control Equipment and Safety Devices.

In most types of equipment, provisions are made for local volume control and for program selection where more than one program is available. These volume controls and channel (program) selectors may be mounted with the loud speaker, or at any convenient place designated. This equipment is also supplied in portable form to be used with an extension cord. The practice in schoolrooms is to place the loud speaker above the level of the top of the blackboard and then locate controls at a height convenient for the teacher—about four feet from the floor. Program selection is accomplished either by the use of plugs and jacks or by means of a rotating selector switch. The latter arrangement is somewhat more convenient and less subject to injury. If the loud speakers are not permanently mounted and particularly if they are not the flush wall type there might be a distinct advantage in using plugs and jacks because the connections could be made and broken easily.

When loud speakers are mounted flush with the wall it is possible to install them so that they cannot be removed or tampered with unless special tools are used. This arrangement removes a great temptation from the pupils. A good way to localize short circuit troubles is to place miniature fuses at each extension. When flush wall type loud speakers are used the over-all protection is simple because the opening from the cone can be covered with a heavy grill and cloth, the remainder of the outfit being enclosed. For loud speakers that are not mounted flush with the wall some strong over-all enclosure should be provided. This enclosure should be so constructed that it will not interfere with proper functioning of the loud speaker and it should be equipped with a lock.

Some manufacturers provide fuses for use in the circuits at each loud speaker. This arrangement is valuable in places where a large number of loud speakers are on the same circuit.

When several dynamic speakers are connected in series across 110 volts AC, the inductive kick is large at the time the circuit is broken. This trouble can be reduced by placing a resistance across each loud speaker.

Loud Speaker Testing Methods.

Practically all of the reproduction characteristics of a loud speaker can be obtained from a frequency-response curve when the tester has worked with enough loud speakers to interpret the results. In order to obtain a frequency-response curve, energy is delivered to the speaker and then the sound energy is measured at selected distances from the speaker for all audible frequencies. Since sound energy is manifest as velocity of air and as air pressure, either or both components of this energy could be measured. A "Rayleigh Disc" could be used for measuring the velocity component while for the pressure component some kind of sensitive microphone could be used. Wolff and Ringel [9] used a small condenser type microphone. Their apparatus consisted of an oscillator which supplied a measured amount of energy at a known frequency to the loud speaker and a condenser microphone connected to an amplifier, detector and recorder. The condenser microphone must be as small as possible in order to prevent distortion of the sound field. From the results obtained, curves are plotted on logarithmic paper. These curves are then interpreted.

The subjective tests described in the section on phonograph

[9] Wolff Irving and Ringel, A. "Loud Speaker Testing Methods." *Proceedings, Institute of Radio Engineers*, Vol. 15, May 1927, pp. 363-76.

pickups are applicable to loud speakers, especially for over-all tests.

The articulation test used by telephone engineers for testing telephone equipment can be used for a test on loud speakers. This test is very good to judge the response the loud speaker is giving to high frequencies. In this test a list of syllables is read and several listeners record the syllables as they are understood. The percentage of syllables correctly understood is taken as a measure of articulation.

Information Needed by an Engineer on Nature of Coverage Required.

Before an engineer can make intelligent recommendations regarding loud speakers for any particular installation he must have exact data on the nature of the coverage desired. Sometimes because of unexpected acoustic difficulties it is necessary to make adjustments after the installation has been made. The engineer or manufacturer should be given information regarding: (1) size and nature of the rooms, halls, auditorium, or outdoor area to be covered; (2) approximate draping or damping effects; (3) number of seats in the room; (4) approximate desired placing of input apparatus; (5) average number of people in the audience; (6) approximate desired type and location of loud speaker apparatus; and (7) volume level desired (excessive or natural volume). It is a great help to the engineer if he is supplied with a complete set of plans of the building in which the installation is to be made.

Number of Loud Speakers Required in Given Situations.

Absorption and other acoustic properties of large rooms play such a large part that it is difficult to determine how many loud speakers of a given type are necessary. The power a given speaker will handle without interfering with the quality of the reproduction and the characteristics of sound projectors as to diffusion of the sound, both must be considered in determining the number of loud speakers needed. Silver says:

It has been found experimentally and confirmed in a number of tests and installations that, assuming a frequency characteristic flat from 80 to 4,000 and 4,500 cycles, a power of 400 to 700 milliwatts (thousandths of a watt) delivered to an average reproducer is adequate to provide home entertainment at volume levels giving a natural impression; from 700 to 800, or possibly 1,000 milliwatts seems desirable for dancing in the average home. These figures apply equally well in practice to magnetic or dynamic speakers for home, school room, or apartment use. For auditoriums and theaters seating 500 to 1,000 people, with all seats occupied, from 3 to 5 watts delivered to one or two reproducers will produce an impression of natural volume. . . . Systems delivering about five watts to two reproducers give adequate coverage of 1,000 to 2,000 seat theaters. For houses of 2,000 seats up, higher powers are needed; from 15 to 30 watts delivered to 4 to 8 speakers being desirable to insure safe reserve capacity for 3,000 to 6,000 seat houses. The above figures contemplate indoor operation, under draped or damped surroundings, and in practice give an impression of naturalness. . . .

For outdoor operation, good coverage for crowds of 10,000 to 15,000 people can be had with 5 watts delivered to 1 to 6 speakers, while 15 watts will make coverage more effective and allow a reserve for unfavorable absorption such as might be encountered in portable work. Thirty watts appears sufficient for crowds of 10,000 to 20,000 or more depending upon the grouping and absorption.[10]

Silver [11] suggests that a good rule of thumb for practical installations is to allow so many watts per loud speaker. He advises allowing 1 to 2 watts for small air-chrome type speakers, or small air-column horns; 2 to 3 watts for large linen diaphragm speakers; and 2 to 4 watts for large baffle (36 to 40 inches square) dynamic projectors.

The following are data given by representatives of the Radio Corporation of America for the loud speakers which they recommend: one magnetic type for rooms having seating capacity of 50 or less, one eight-inch cone dynamic type for a room with seating capacity of 50 to 200, two for 200 to 500, three for 500 to 750, and six for 1,500.

WIRING AND CONDUIT SYSTEMS FOR AUDIO FREQUENCY DISTRIBUTION

The wiring and conduit system referred to here connects the sound reproducers (loud speakers and head phones) with the amplifying equipment. The electrical power transmitted over these wires is very small when thought of in terms of the power used by an ordinary electric light. The power required to operate a good moving coil loud speaker is about 4 watts while the small electric lamps commonly used in a home consume 50 watts or

---

[10] Silver, McMurdo. "Some Practical Data on Public Address Amplification." *Radio Engineering*, Vol. 8 (December 1928), No. 12, p. 27.
[11] *Ibid.,* p. 28.

more. The size of the wires required for audio frequency distribution causes no particular trouble because any good conductor which is strong enough to be pulled through the conduit will have sufficient current-carrying capacity for this work. Different companies specify sizes of wire ranging from Number 19 up to Number 14, B and S gauge. The current-carrying capacity of the Number 14 wire is far beyond that required; it is specified primarily because it is mechanically stronger than the smaller wires. Large wires are preferable on long runs when low impedance is desired.

To avoid the ordinary inductance and capacity effects it is common practice to specify that the wires of each pair be twisted together. These are referred to commercially as twisted pairs. It is also common to specify that the wire be rubber-covered and braided. When several pairs of wires carrying different programs (different channels) are placed in the same conduit, provision must be made to prevent inductive interference (cross talk) between the circuits. This calls for shielding. If the shielding is to be complete the circuits must be entirely enclosed in a good conductor. The regular rigid iron conduit will act as a shield if the joints are so soldered as to be totally enclosing and if only one pair of wires passes through it. The same is true of metal raceways, flexible metallic conduit, and steel armored cable. When several channels are placed in the same conduit it is essential that the channels be shielded from each other. Two common methods of providing for shielding are: using lead-covered twin conductors; using special audio frequency wire. It is always best to provide adequate shielding even if only one channel is installed because the system will be flexible; additional channels can be added at any time as long as the capacity of the conduit is not exceeded. Theoretically it is not necessary to provide shielding for one of the pairs of wires if the other pairs are shielded. Telephone engineers require that the voltage induced in Circuit A by Circuit B shall not be more than one-tenth the normal voltage in Circuit A.

It is the general practice to run several trunk lines from the central station and then take short branches from these. Vertical trunk lines are employed in tall buildings while horizontal trunk lines serve the purpose in low buildings. It has been found distinctly advantageous to group the outlets (loud speaker or head

phones) on circuits and then to run each circuit back to the
central station into a cut-off switch which opens both sides of the
circuit. These circuits usually carry about ten loud speakers.
This arrangement makes it simpler to service the system since
trouble can be quickly localized. The exact wiring layout depends upon the kind of service desired and the room arrangement
in the building. In some places the auditorium equipment is
entirely separate from the central station equipment. When a
separate pair of signal wires extends from each loud speaker
to the control board, it is possible to make direct connection with
one loud speaker without disturbing any other loud speaker.
Many engineers recommend that the branch circuits be run in at
least one-half inch conduits and it is better to use three-fourths
inch ones to provide for future extension. The size of the conduit
is determined as soon as the circuits have been laid out. The
National Electric Code [12] specifies the number of wires to be
carried in any conduit of given size. If sheathing is used, larger
conduit will be required for a given number of wires. It is
economical to allow enough space in the conduit for at least one
extra channel to provide for future expansion. In fact, a still
better practice is to include the wiring for the extra channel when
the original installation is made.

Central Rack and Panels

The control panels referred to here should have provisions for
monitoring, load segregation, and testing. Control panels are
built which make it possible by the use of plugs and jacks or
selector switches to connect any distribution line to a test loud
speaker, meters, or other testing equipment. All of the separate
circuits end at this panel. The output from the amplifiers is fed
into this panel and thence distributed to any circuits desired.
When several distinct amplifier systems feed into the panel,
provision is made to place the output from any amplifier or any
distribution circuit. Where the audio frequency distribution
wiring system is such that separate service to individual rooms
is possible then the control panel has provisions for selecting
any particular room or group of rooms. In cases of this kind
the service arrangements are similar to those in the distribution

[12] *National Electric Code,* pp. 42-43. Regulations of the National Board of Fire Underwriters for Electric Wiring and Apparatus, 1928 Edition.

board of the clock and bell program systems. If the loud speakers are to be used as microphones, provision must be made on the control board to switch the circuit from the loud speaker into the input of the amplifying system.

Some control panels carry all the indicating instruments as well as the devices for controlling the volume output into each circuit. The panels also carry the power switches, transfer switches for various kinds of service (radio, microphone, phonograph), program selectors for the radio service, fuses and other types of equipment depending upon the elaborateness of the installation. Some installations have automatic time switches which turn the outfit on and off at definite times and, with locking devices, the controls and selectors can be maintained in a fixed position.

The central rack includes a number of panels for each channel. The practice in building the racks is to make them tall, but not broad or deep. The dimensions of one typical rack are $20\frac{1}{2}''$ wide $\times$ $18\frac{3}{4}''$ deep $\times$ $6'10\frac{7}{8}''$ high. The rack and panels are so related in design that there is great freedom in placing the panels on the racks. Panels can be replaced or interchanged without much work. Space is always left on a rack for a sufficient number of additional panels to care for any reasonable future demands on the system. For each additional channel a duplicate rack must be added.

When power is obtained from storage batteries or motor-generator sets with proper filters, additional panels are usually required. A charging panel is commonly installed with the storage batteries. The motor generator requires some place to locate the starting equipment. It is not necessary to place the storage batteries or the motor generator at the same place or even in the same room with the control equipment. In fact, it is generally better not to have them in the same room, especially the motor generator. Obviously the distance between the source of power and the remainder of the equipment should be made as small as possible in order to minimize the line losses.

The following points must be considered when deciding upon the location of the central station equipment: (1) nearness to power supply; (2) protection from unauthorized meddling; (3) advisable termination of radio distribution lines and antenna lead-in; (4) who will possibly operate the system; (5) proximity to elevator shafts and other disturbing equipment; (6) the uses which are to be made of the equipment; and (7) accessibility to the operator.

Several places in the school building are favorable. Probably the best place to locate the central station equipment, from the standpoint of supervision, is in the principal's office or in a small room adjoining. This location is good from nearly every standpoint, especially in low buildings. The principal's clerk might operate the set. For technical reasons it is better to locate the equipment on the top floor in a tall building. Another favorable location for the central station is in a small room at the side of the stage in the auditorium. This location is not quite so desirable as the others suggested from the standpoint of accessibility to the principal; however, it has other advantages which cannot be disregarded. In this position the station can be operated without disturbing the office routine and it is near the microphones used to pick up the programs to be broadcast to other rooms or to be amplified for the audience in the same room. In fact, many of the portable and semiportable outfits are actually located in this position. Wherever the station is located it should be in an enclosure which can be locked.

Some engineers believe there is an advantage in shielding the room containing the amplifiers and other central station equipment. One plan suggested was to use one-fourth or three-eighths inch copper mesh in the place of the metal lath ordinarily used. If shielding is undertaken it is essential that provision be made for the shielding currents to flow where they will. This means that there must be no unsoldered joints in the shielding. To shield the equipment completely from outside electric and magnetic effects it is necessary to enclose the equipment in the most perfect conductor obtainable. The expense involved in providing a good shield is quite large. For this reason, and also because most of the serious disturbing electric and magnetic effects are picked up by the antenna system, room shielding has not been advocated.

Audio Frequency Transformers

Good transformers are essential in any audio frequency distribution system. Improvements in transformer construction are made continually. One of the outstanding differences between the old transformers and the new ones is revealed in the reproduction of low tones. The quality of an audio frequency transformer is measured by its ability to amplify signals uniformly and to reproduce low frequency bass notes of the order of 25 to 30 cycles and harmonics sufficiently high to cover the more important portion of the audible range. The function of the audio frequency transformer is to amplify and pass on to the next stage the delicate signals from the detector tube. The output transformer provides a connection between the plate circuit of the last tube of the amplifier and the loud speaker. Transformers must be built to match the tubes with which they are to be used. The greater the primary impedance of the transformer relative to the plate impedance of the tube, the larger will be the voltage in the primary coil; hence, the greater the amplification. Impedance changes in the same ratio as the frequency.

Good transformers must have the proper amount of grid bias. Without grid bias the best transformers are no better than the poorest. With the right amount of grid bias the grid is so negative to start with that the positive half of the wave never makes it positive, no grid current ever flows, and both halves of the wave are amplified alike. A good transformer unit should not require any additional resistances or condensers across the primary or secondary terminals.

The push-pull transformer and tube arrangement is extremely useful in obtaining large sound volume without distortion. The grid voltage swing resulting from a given signal input is divided between two tubes by means of a center tap on the audio transformer. The center tap is connected with a common grid bias. This arrangement provides for a double signal without distortion. Even harmonics due to tube distortion are neutralized in the primary of the output transformer. Odd harmonics appear only when the tubes are heavily overloaded.

With the advent of the demand for the reproduction of low tones the use of an output transformer becomes practically a necessity. In most cases this transformer is required and many of the best radio engineers believe that in all cases its use is advisable. One reason for the use of the transformer is that such a device is generally necessary to provide a connection between the plate current of the last tube of the amplifier and the loud speaker so that the best results will be obtained on both low and high notes. Furthermore, the transformer eliminates direct current from the windings of the loud speaker. The direct current goes through the primary of the transformer and the loud speaker receives only the varying current of the secondary of the transformer, thus protecting the loud speaker magnets and the delicate windings of the loud speaker as well as keeping the dangerous plate voltages away from the operator. The transformer relieves the magnetic stress on the moving or vibrating element of the loud speaker. This element can then travel farther and more freely with the result that greater volume can be obtained without distortion and rattling. A transformer is preferable to a capacity-choke because the time constant is less; hence, a more faithful reproduction of the impact notes is possible.

Amplifiers

The possible output from a distribution system is determined to a large degree by the characteristics of the amplifying system. While the principal function of the amplifier is to increase the strength of the signal it also plays a very important part in determining the quality and range of the reproduced sounds. The over-all amplification of a complete unit should be sufficient to boost the weakest signal to the full output of the system. The input signals from different sources have different strengths, consequently the amplifiers must be built to match the kind of input equipment used. According to Silver [13] the average radio set detector tube produces an audio signal voltage of 0.3 volts without distortion, the average magnetic record pickup produces one volt, and the average double-button carbon microphone produces 0.05 volts or less in actual use. With two 250-type tubes connected in push-pull in the output stage and with approximately 15 watts output at maximum voltage the voltage gain (amplification) needed for the radio detector would be 260, for the magnetic pickup 79, and for the microphone 1,580. In addition to increasing the volume of the signal the amplifier must reproduce this signal faithfully, distortion must be held at a minimum. Ideally the signals should be strengthened without any distortion. In some radio sets the vibration of the baffle board is depended upon for low tones. This is bad practice

[13] Silver, *op. cit.*, p. 29.

because it is upon the characteristics of the electrical amplifier system that reproduction of low tones depends.

In radio reception two distinctly different types of amplifiers are used, depending upon the frequency of the currents and voltages to be amplified. One type is known as the high frequency amplifier. This type of amplifier is used where the incoming high frequency currents and voltages are first strengthened and then reduced in frequency. The other type is known as the low frequency amplifier. In this case the currents and voltages are strengthened after they have been reduced in frequency. High frequency amplification is used in centralized systems only in the radio receiver.

For use with centralized systems, amplifiers are now furnished in units, each unit having definite characteristics. These units are often built to fit in a series and then designated as primary, secondary, etc. Some companies manufacture the units as input amplifiers and output amplifiers. The last amplifier in the series is generally known as the power amplifier. In practically all modern distribution systems the push-pull (explained under transformers) connection of matched power tubes is employed. Each amplifier unit is built to operate a certain number of loud speakers or head phones at certain volume levels. For instance, if one model amplifier is rated to operate a maximum of 30 schoolroom loud speakers, additional service can be obtained by adding a duplicate amplifier for each 30 loud speakers. In another arrangement a certain amplifier will operate 32 loud speakers at normal talking intensities while the addition of another amplifier of different design fed by the first one will operate 200 loud speakers at the same intensity. It is evident that these arrangements make for great flexibility. The number of loud speakers which can be accommodated in either case depends upon the characteristics of the loud speakers and upon the volume levels desired. Some manufacturers supply an amplifying system which will operate a large number (200 in one case) of loud speakers at normal speaking intensities and then provide taps on the output transformers of the amplifier units so that different volume levels can be obtained, simultaneously if desired. It is always important to know what undistorted power the amplifiers can develop. When the system is made up of units this characteristic should be known for each unit in order to avoid overloading. Provisions are generally made for connecting monitor or test loud speakers and for shutting off the loud speakers without affecting the monitoring circuit.

It is advisable in furnishing the power supply to the amplifier tubes to delay turning on the plate current for a short time after the filament current has been turned on. This precaution is essential when working with amplifiers which use much power. In order to remove the human element which is so important in manual controls some manufacturers are introducing time-lag relays for this service. The use of a time-lag relay for this service is very convenient in places where remote controls are employed.

Transmitters (Microphones)

In a centralized system the transmitter has one function in common with the phonograph pickup and the radio pickup; namely, to furnish input signals to the amplifiers. The transmitter picks up power from an acoustic system and delivers power to an electric system, the wave form in the two systems being the same in an ideal transmitter.

There are two common types of transmitters (microphones): carbon transmitters and condenser transmitters. Carbon transmitters are subdivided into two groups: the ordinary single-button transmitter and the double-button transmitter. Single-button carbon transmitters are common in hand sets used for making announcements. Double-button carbon transmitters and condenser transmitters are used for broadcasting work of all kinds.

The single-button carbon transmitter can handle only small currents without the development of arcs between the carbon granules. It is used primarily for close-talking service. In most announcing outfits it has been replaced by the double-button transmitter. The maximum allowable motion of the diaphragm is about .001 inch if the output current is to be like the sound pressure wave input.

The double-button carbon transmitter produces twice the effect that the single-button carbon transmitter does. The former is sturdy and the current generated does not magnetize the core. The double-button transmitter consists of a thin, stretched metal diaphragm on each side of which is mounted a carbon transmitter button. The carbon buttons are connected in push-pull arrangement, so that the current on one side increases when that on the other side decreases. The diaphragm is tightly stretched and is placed a short distance from a metal plate. The stretching causes a high period for the diaphragm and the metal plate makes for high damping. These reduce the sensitivity; consequently, more amplification is required. Broadcasting microphones must be very insensitive (about 1/100 the sensitivity of an ordinary telephone) to get faithful reproduction. Morecroft, Pinto and Curry [14] say that about five millivolts are generated by a double-button carbon microphone under the influence of a sound wave pressure of one dyne per square centimeter.

The condenser transmitter is the most nearly perfect transmitter in use to-day. It is hard, however, to have the leakage current negligible compared with the charging current. Damp weather causes varying leakage and makes the transmitter noisy. In fact, all types of transmitters must be protected from dampness. The condenser transmitter consists of a thin metal diaphragm (usually steel or duralumin) tightly stretched in front of a perfectly flat plate and spaced .001 inch from the plate. The outside air is excluded from the space between the plate and the diaphragm. The variations in atmospheric pressure are taken care of by a compensating diaphragm at the rear of the plate. One side of the compensating diaphragm is in contact with the outside air, the other side through holes in the plate. The operation of this transmitter depends upon the variation in the capacity between the diaphragm and the back plate when the diaphragm is vibrated by sound waves. The variations in capacity cause variations in the voltage which the unit will take. The resulting varying voltage through a resistance is supplied to the grid of the amplifier.

Transmitters of the better types must be mounted to receive a minimum of mechanical vibration. These mountings are designed with their eventual location—on tables, on the floor, or suspended from the ceiling—in mind. It is customary to place the transmitter amplifier in the mounting. Base outlets for the double-button carbon transmitters should have three connections and for condenser transmitters five connections.

When loud speakers are used in the same room with the trans-

[14] Morecroft, Pinto and Curry, *op. cit.*, p. 752.

mitters the latter should be placed well behind a line crossing the loud speaker faces or radiating openings. The following are some instructions given by the Western Electric Company relative to locating transmitters: [15]

1. The leads from the input to the amplifier should be connected to permanently located receptacles and plugs should be attached to the end of the transmitter leads.
2. Transmitter leads should not be near power lines.
3. A speaker or a soloist should be two to six feet from the front of the transmitters (readers must watch so that the papers from which they read do not block the transmitter).
4. To pick up piano music the transmitter should be a few feet from the instrument and it should face the keyboard.
5. For picking up music from an orchestra the transmitter should be over the orchestra and somewhat in front, and near the strings and basses.
6. For large organizations several transmitters may be required. These should feed into a grouping mixing panel.
7. To pick up phonograph music the transmitter should be placed diagonally in front of the instrument.

Phonograph Pickup and Associated Equipment *

The function of the phonograph pickup is to pick up electrically that which the ordinary phonograph diaphragm picks up mechanically. The alternating current thus set up is impressed upon the amplifying system where its amplitude is increased many times before it is delivered to the loud speakers.

The operation of the phonograph pickup is in accordance with the phenomenon that a changing magnetic flux linking the turns of a coil will induce an electromotive force (that force which causes the current to flow) in the coil. In the ordinary types of phonograph pickups the changes in the magnetic flux linking the coil are accomplished by having an armature pivoted so that it will rock between the poles of a fixed magnet. The armature, which is usually a bundle of iron wires, offers comparatively low resistance to the magnetic flux; consequently, the magnetic field is distorted so that as many magnetic lines of force as possible will pass through the armature. The position of the armature relative to the pole pieces of the permanent magnet influences

---

[15] Western Electric Company. *General Information for the Care and Operation of a Public Address System*, Instruction Bulletin, No. 177.

* Otherwise known as magnetic pickup, electromagnetic pickup, and electromagnetic reproducer.

decidedly the direction the lines of force will take. The phonograph needle is firmly fastened to the armature. The motion of the armature is produced when the needle follows the markings on the phonograph record. The most common ways of mounting the coils are: (1) the coil is placed in a fixed position in slots in the pole pieces of the permanent magnet; (2) the coil is wound around the armature. In the first arrangement the change in magnetic flux through the coil is produced by the change in the characteristics of the magnetic field between the poles of the magnet caused by the shifting of the position of the armature alone. In the second case, both the armature and the coil shift.

If both hill-and-dale (Edison) and lateral cut type (Victor, Brunswick, Columbia, etc.) records are to be used care must be taken to see that the pickup will operate on both types of records. Most of the phonograph pickups are built for use with the lateral cut type records. The Thomas A. Edison Company has added recently the lateral cut type of records to its line. Because of present tendencies in record manufacture there is little need for provision for the hill-and-dale type records.

Rating Phonograph Pickups and Associated Equipment.

The most important test used to determine the quality of a phonograph pickup and its associated equipment is that which reveals the output from the system at a large number of frequencies throughout the musical scale. For this purpose two methods are in use: subjective—judgment of several listeners; objective—accurate laboratory measurements.

Objective Test for Output.

For these tests a set of constant frequency records is used. The Victor abbreviated set is convenient because many frequencies are recorded on the same record. These records are known as the "Aural Test Set"; the catalogue numbers are 84517, 84518, 84519, and 83001. Each frequency is recorded on a sufficiently large part of the records that the other necessary measurements can be made while the tone is being produced. These records give correction factors for the output for each frequency in terms of that for 1,000 cycles per second. The results can then be interpreted in the way they would be judged by a listener. The steps in the test are: (1) set the volume control for the phonograph-amplifier system at or near the position for maximum output; (2) insert a Victor extra loud Tungs-tone needle or stylus to full depth in the magnetic pickup; (3) place this needle so that it will follow the tracing for one of the constant frequencies and measure the voltage output of the associated amplifying system. The voltage is measured across a resistance in the output circuit of the amplifier. This resistance must be equal to the plate resistance of the output tube. Repeat the entire process for each of a number of frequencies above and below 1,000 cycles per second. Then apply the correction factors given on the constant frequency records and plot a curve between output voltage and frequency.

Subjective Test for Output.

For this test it is necessary to have a sound radiator like a loud speaker in addition to the magnetic pickup and amplifier. In fact, the addition of the loud speaker is desirable because the subjective tests are made primarily to determine the over-all characteristics of the set. In practice the tests are really comparison tests in which one outfit is compared with another. Sometimes the output of the outfits is compared with the reproductions of the same records by high class phonographs like the Orthophonic Victrola. These phonographs are so much alike that they serve as good standards for comparison. Where these tests are made on a large scale the listeners are so experienced that they do not need a standard set with which to compare the test set. They know exactly what characteristics are common to good sets as well as the outstanding defects of poor sets. Where several sets are compared the identity of the sets must not be revealed to the listener until the test has been completed.

In order to get the greatest benefit from a test of this kind the set should be operated in the surroundings and under the conditions in which it is to be used. If it is to be a part of the central station equipment of a program system then it should be tested as an integral part of that equipment. When these tests are performed by other than trained testers it is well to include in the audience people who have a keen appreciation of good tone quality. The judgment of good musicians is invaluable.

One of the most important items of equipment for a test of this kind is a good set of records. These records should be representative of all the kinds which are likely to be used when the set is in service. Furthermore, the records should be chosen with the idea of having present a wide variety of pitches covering as nearly as possible the entire musical range. Particular care should be taken to get records which have recorded tones of those frequencies which are hard to reproduce, those of very low frequency (100 and below) and those of high frequency (3,000 and above). The following is a carefully selected list [16] of records now being used for this kind of test work by the employees of one of the largest producers of electric phonographs:

Character and Name of Record	Victor Record Number 1928 Catalogue
Orchestral:	
Concert: Hungarian Rhapsody	6652
Concert: Toccata and Fugue	6751
Concert: El Capitan	20191
Concert (with tenor): I Pagliacci	1183
Dance: Idolizing	20270
The Calinda	20882
Instrumental:	
Violin and Organ: War March	35873
Piano: Rustle of Spring	20121
Violin: Hebrew Melody	6695
Vocal:	
Soprano: Il Bacio	1262
Male Voices: Lost Chord	35806
Tenor: I Pagliacci	6754

A very accurate check on the reproduction of tones within a given frequency range could be obtained with the aid of a special type of constant frequency record. These records should be prepared so that each frequency is recorded with such amplitude that when accurately reproduced all the frequencies will sound equally loud. When this type of record is used, the listener can judge the output characteristics of the equipment by observing those frequencies which are accentuated or repressed.

Scratch or Surface Noises.

It is extremely important that provision be made for eliminating scratch or surface noises without too great sacrifice of the frequencies near the scratch frequencies. When powerful ampli-

[16] List furnished by Mr. T. R. Bunting, Technical and Test Department, Radio Corporation of America.

fiers are used with the phonograph pickup the need for good scratch filters is more evident. Scratch noises are easily detected when tests like those outlined above are carried out.

Wear on the Phonograph Record.

A phonograph pickup is quite inferior if in its operation it is very destructive to the record. Sometimes the action of the armature is so stiff that the tracings on the record are reamed out or otherwise destroyed. This trouble can be minimized by providing for a certain degree of freedom of motion of the part which holds the needle.

Motor Speed Control.

Since the pitch of a tone varies directly with the frequency, the faster a record is rotated the higher the pitch will be. It is therefore necessary for the record to be rotated at a nearly consistent speed, if the reproduced notes are to have the proper tone relationship. Stoller makes the following statement regarding the allowable speed variation:

In determining how nearly constant this (speed) should be held, the criterion is the smallest pitch change that is noticeable, and it has been found that abrupt variations are more readily perceived than slow ones. A good musical ear will detect sudden changes in pitch produced by a change in speed of only one-half of one per cent. To make sure, therefore, that a discernible change in pitch never arises, speed regulation better than one-half of one per cent is required at all times. As further allowances seemed desirable to provide a suitable factor of safety, a regulation of two-tenths of one per cent was agreed upon.[17]

Radio Receiver

As used in most centralized systems, the radio receiver includes an associated amplifier besides the amplifiers used for the whole system. Certain characteristics will be mentioned here which are definitely associated with the amplifier section of the unit. The function of the radio receiver is to pick up radio signals and place them on the amplifying system. Radio receivers applicable to school work may be designed to pick up either long wave (low frequency) or short wave (high frequency) or both. Long wave receivers are designed to pick up those frequencies which lie in the ordinary broadcast range. The frequency band allotted to

[17] Stoller Hugh M. "Speed Control for the Sound Picture System." *Bell Laboratories Record*, November 1928.

broadcasting in the United States ranges from 500 to 1,500 kilocycles. Within this range the frequencies upon which the individual stations operate must be separated from each other by ten kilocycles. Each station is allowed to deviate from its authorized frequency by not more than 500 cycles. There are many stations now operating that maintain their frequencies within 100 cycles. The short wave receivers which operate in the neighborhood of twenty meters are now used primarily for extremely long distance work. Because of the growing interest in short wave reception, many manufacturers are placing receiving sets on the market which have provisions for both long and short wave reception.

So much development work has been done on radio receivers that there are now many good sets on the market. As new types of vacuum tubes are developed new types of receiving sets are built around them. In the earlier sets crystals served the purpose now universally served by vacuum tubes. Within recent years provisions have been made so that the electric power supply can be taken directly from the house lighting circuit instead of from storage cells or dry cells. Commercially, the sets are said to be electric. Some designers still prefer the storage cells service of power for certain parts of the equipment where a steady power supply is needed. It is necessary for the purchaser to know whether his electric lighting power supply is alternating current or direct current, because the receivers are built to operate on one or the other.

Many high-class receivers are available, and since their designers employ so many different methods for obtaining desired results the next few paragraphs will be devoted to discussing some outstanding characteristics by which receivers are judged. Some tentative standards and tests against which to check characteristics in a receiver will be given also. Some tests require elaborate equipment and skilled operators. However, the time has come when purchasers insist upon more accurate information regarding the equipment which they buy. To meet this demand at least one company (The General Radio Company) is now placing on the market an instrument for testing some of the most important performance characteristics of a receiver. The discussion of sensitivity, selectivity, fidelity, and volume control follows:

Sensitivity.

The Committee on Standards [18] of the Institute of Radio Engineers has defined sensitivity as "the degree to which a radio receiving set responds to signals of the frequency to which it is tuned." The layman thinks of sensitivity as the ability a set has of bringing in distant stations. High amplification, particularly of the radio frequencies, enables the set to bring in these distant stations. Sensitivity is a distinct asset if it can be attained without instability which impairs quality. The instability generally manifests itself in the tendency toward self-oscillation of one or more of the tubes. Some receivers have sensitivity controls that permit the operator to vary the sensitivity and thus minimize atmospheric and other disturbances originating at points more distant than the station being received. Increased sensitivity in receivers using an indoor antenna has been accomplished by using several stages of tuned radio frequency. It is very important to consider the place in which a receiving set is to be used. If there are many high-class broadcasting stations near by, it is far more important to be able to obtain one desired station at a time and exclude the others than it is to be able to pick up distant stations. The reverse is true if the receiver is to be used in a place where all good broadcasting stations are far away.

The following are some reasonable, tentative standards proposed by Mr. E. T. Dickey of the Technical and Test Department of the Radio Corporation of America.[19] These standards were determined by considering the present development of the art of radio communication. For a receiver of high sensitivity a normal power output of 0.05 watts should be obtained with thirty microvolts on the receiving antenna per meter effective height of the antenna. A set with poor sensitivity should give the normal signal with 200 microvolts on the receiving antenna per meter effective height.

The following are the essentials of a test outlined by Mr. C. C. Shumard, also of the Technical and Test Department of the Radio Corporation of America, for checking a set against the above standards:

[18] Committee on Standards, Institute of Radio Engineers. *Definition of Terms and Graphic Symbols*, 1926.
[19] Personal interview.

Keep the power input constant at 0.05 watts. Find the electric field strength required to produce this output from the receiver at a number of frequencies within the broadcast range. A dummy antenna is used for this test. Set the tube oscillator at the frequency desired and then tune set to this frequency. Adjust the receiver by manipulation of the oscillator and attenuator so that receiver outfit is 0.05 watts. Repeat for all frequencies at which the sensitivity is desired. Plot the results on rectangular coördinate paper with input microvolts per meter as ordinate, and wave length in kilocycles as abscissa.[20]

For further details on this test and other tests that follow the reader is referred to the Preliminary Report of a Committee on Standards for the Institute of Radio Engineers, May, 1928, and later reports which may be published by this committee. The 1928 Preliminary Report is published in the NEMA Handbook of Radio Standards.[21] Tests of a similar nature are outlined in an article by Hull [22] explaining the use of the General Radio Company's equipment.

Selectivity.

The selectivity of a receiver is a measure of how little the reception of signals from a certain transmitting station are interfered with by the presence of electromagnetic waves of different wave lengths or frequencies emanating from other stations. The Institute of Radio Engineers' [23] definition is: "The degree to which a radio receiving set responds to signals of the frequencies to which it is tuned." Some engineers express the selectivity in terms of the field strength required to produce a given power output when the receiver is in tune and out of tune with the incoming signal. One manufacturer specifies that for frequencies 10 kilocycles removed from any radio frequency a radio field strength three times that of the resonance (tuned) frequency field strength shall be necessary to produce the same power output.

It is possible to have the selectivity too great for practical use. In these cases there would be excessively sharp tuning, technically known as "side band cutting." The top of the response curve for a very selective receiver would be quite

---

[20] Personal interview.

[21] National Electrical Manufacturers Association. *Handbook of Radio Standards, Fourth Edition,* pp. 89-141, New York, 1928.

[22] Hull, L. M. "Over-all Measurements on Broadcast Receivers." *Proceedings of the Radio Club of America,* Vol. 5 (October 1928), No. 8, pp. 85-93.

[23] *Preliminary Report of a Committee on Standards for the Institute of Radio Engineers,* May 1928.

sharp. Since broadcast stations are allowed 500 cycles' variation in their broadcast wave frequencies, the top of the response curve of the receiver should be broad enough that all of the frequencies emitted from the transmitting station can be equally amplified. If this provision is not made, the quality of the reproduction will suffer. It is true that the high-class broadcasting stations do keep the variation in frequencies of the transmitted waves as much as one-fifth or less than at present allowed by the Federal Radio Commission.

The apparent selectivity of a receiver decreases as the sensitivity increases and vice versa. Of two sets having equal actual selectivity the one with the higher sensitivity will seem broader or less selective. It is therefore important to balance selectivity and sensitivity in such a way that set performance produced is best suited to the particular kind of service desired. For ordinary receiving conditions the engineer strives for maximum selectivity with reasonable sensitivity. If the receiver is to be used where broadcast stations are far away it is better to sacrifice some selectivity in order to get more distance.

The following are standards proposed by Dickey for receivers of three levels of selectivity. The term "width" used in these standards means the number of kilocycles of radio frequency between a frequency below that for which the set is tuned and one above this resonant frequency where the electric field strength in the antenna (microvolts per meter) is 100 times that required to produce an output from the set equal to the original output for the resonant frequency.

For high selectivity there should be approximately thirty kilocycles width at all points of the broadcast range. For medium selectivity the maximum width at 1,400 kilocycles should be 120 kilocycles, and at 600 kilocycles it should be forty kilocycles. For poorest acceptable selectivity the maximum width at 1,400 kilocycles should be 230 kilocycles, and at 600 kilocycles it should be 90 kilocycles.

The test outlined below and any others given in the treatment referred to under "sensitivity" will serve to check the selectivity of a receiver. The essentials of the selectivity test as outlined by Shumard follow: adjust the output from the set to approximately 0.05 watts (normal output) while tuned to a certain frequency, say 600 kilocycles; vary this radio frequency produced by the oscillator in steps of five or ten kilocycles above and below the frequency to which the set is tuned. By means of the attenuator, or the oscillator output, or both bring the receiver to the starting value for each step. Calculate the field strength in microvolts per meter in the antenna. Keeping the output constant, vary the frequency below and above that to which the receiver is tuned until a frequency is obtained which requires a field strength 100 times that necessary at the tuning frequency. Plot the field strength as ordinates and radio frequency as abscissa using a log scale for the ordinates. Repeat this entire process for each resonant frequency. Subtract the lower limit frequency obtained by this process from the upper limit frequency to get "width" referred to under standards above at each of the resonant frequencies.

Fidelity.

Applied to radio receiver characteristics, fidelity means the faithfulness with which the unit reproduces the signals transmitted to it from the sending station. The fidelity of reproduction is noticeable to a listener only when a reproducer is associated with the receiver so that sound sensations can be perceived. It is then manifest in the quality of the tones emitted. It is absolutely essential that the receiver and the reproducer be matched if good tone quality is to result. Loss in fidelity is occasioned primarily by a change in a wave; for instance, in passing through a circuit or transmission medium. This change is technically known as distortion. Distortion may be caused by any of the following conditions: (1) the presence in the output of components having frequencies not present in the original wave— the result of the circuit elements not having linear characteristics; (2) a change in the relative amplitudes of the component frequencies, because of variation in the transmission frequency over the frequency range involved; (3) a change in the relative phase of the component frequencies. The last does not cause distortion when present in audio frequency waves.

The following standards for fidelity were proposed by Dickey as reasonable on the basis of the performances of many receiving sets of many makes. For a receiver to be ranked high on fidelity 70 to 80 per cent of the response at 400 cycles should be obtained at 100 cycles and 30 per cent of the response at 400 cycles should be obtained at 3,000 cycles. For all other sets a minimum of 40 per cent of the response at 400 cycles should be obtained at 100 cycles and 30 per cent of the response at 400 cycles should be obtained at 3,000 cycles.

The following are the essentials of a test for over-all fidelity as outlined by Shumard:

Tune the set to the radio frequency at which the fidelity curve is desired. Modulate with audio frequency 30 per cent or any other percentage which will not result in overloading the tube. Adjust the output of the receiver by manipulating the oscillator and the audio frequency input to any convenient value which does not overload the tubes. Vary the audio frequency keeping the input voltage constant with 30 per cent modulation. Record the voltage output of receiver for desired audio frequency. Plot output audio voltage in percentage of that at 400 cycles (ordinates) versus modulating frequency in cycles per second (abscissa). Use a logarithmic scale for the abscissa.

Further treatment of tests for fidelity is given in the references listed in connection with the sensitivity tests.

Volume Control.

The function of the volume control is to regulate the intensity or energy level of the output signal. When the signals have passed through a reproducer the variations in volume are manifest to the listener as changes in loudness. It is essential that changes in volume be made in small enough steps to produce an effect of smooth variation. Many different types of manual volume controls are used in the different commercial sets. In fact, some new radio receivers have automatic volume controls which maintain the volume output constant though the broadcast signal may vary in strength. Some of these automatic controls are said to operate so that the receiver will give equal output with the distant and local stations, and, to a certain extent, take care of fading. The volume-control device should be such that its operation will not produce distortion.

Dickey believes that it is reasonable to expect the volume control to be capable of reducing the output to one-tenth the normal output when the field strength on the antenna is 100 microvolts per meter.

The following test outlined by Shumard may be used to check the performance of a volume control:

Obtain the sensitivity of the receiver as described above with the volume control set for maximum output and then for 90 per cent, 80 per cent, etc., of maximum until the entire volume control is thrown in. The values obtained for all the settings will show the operation of the control throughout its range while the last value will provide the data necessary for checking the standard given for this characteristic (the maximum volume control).

THE ANTENNA AND LEAD-IN EQUIPMENT

It is the function of the antenna (aërial) to pick up the signals which travel through the air. There are many types of antennæ; the essential constructional differences lie in the way the wires are arranged. The inverted L and the loop types are most common. Intensity of signals received by a coil antenna is low compared with the intensity of those received by the inverted L type. However, static interference is less in the latter. The loop responds most vigorously to signals coming from directions in the plane of the coils. The inverted L type is somewhat directional also; it is customary to point the angle of the antenna in the direction of the location of those broadcast stations from which programs are desired. The best antenna should absorb little energy from waves longer than those for which it is tuned. In general, loop antennæ are not favored for use in buildings where there is much steel construction. For this reason, and because the signals are weak in the loop antennæ, most engineers prefer the vertical lead-in and the "ground." On tall buildings the effective ground is sometimes 30 feet or more above the surface of the ground upon which the building rests. In order to minimize the effect of power lines the antenna should be placed as far as possible away from them, and in the case of open power lines it is best to have the antenna set at right angles to them. It is not a good practice to put the antenna near elevators. The antenna should be clear by a generous margin, say twenty feet, of conducting objects such as structural steel, trees, guys, and metal roofs. A long antenna may be used when it is installed where there are no interfering broadcast stations. Where local broadcast stations do interfere the trouble may be relieved by setting the receiver antenna at right angles to the antenna of the broadcaster. Some engineers believe that it is better to keep the antenna length somewhere near normal because it will fit the broadcast range. Longer antennæ are not so selective as shorter ones. Special antenna controls which allow for a wide variation in the antenna system are available. Unless special provisions are made for a radio frequency distribution system, it is best to provide a separate antenna for each channel; that is, there should be as many antennæ as there are radio programs received simultaneously. Some installations have been made in schools where lead-ins were taken off at the several floor levels from a single vertical antenna. In this arrangement the potential is divided and interference with the programs is quite likely. If the light socket aërial is used care must be taken that the device is designed properly. Unless the proper coupling condenser is included in such a device, there is not only a marked loss in signal strength, but also the danger of condenser breakdown or short circuited condenser, resulting in a damaged radio set.

When an outside antenna is used there must be a connecting circuit (lead-in) between the receiving set and the antenna proper. In reality the lead-in is a part of the antenna system and must be so considered in determining the effective length of the antenna. The vertical lead-in and the horizontal part of the antenna are usually one continuous conductor; if not continuous the junction must be firmly soldered in order to assure a good electrical connection. Crooks and turns in the lead-in wire should be avoided wherever possible. A grounded metal conduit or any other metallic covering around the lead-in wire introduces capacity effects. Most radio engineers do not favor their use; however, one engineer interviewed by the writer does favor the use of metal conduit with the lead-in wire in order to cut down the effective length of the antenna. Unless special radio frequency signal amplification is used the preferred practice is to pass the lead-ins through a fibre conduit or else to use no conduit and keep the wire on the outside of the building. On an installation of the latter type the wire is kept clear of the building by several inches and when the desired floor level has been reached the wire is brought in through the wall through insulators so inclined that water cannot drain into the room. The outside lead-in wire is adaptable to use in school installations because the buildings are not high enough to make the run to the receiver excessive. The lead-in wire should be brought down along the building in such a position as to be free from interference of power lines, parallel conductors, and the like. Where there is much loss in the strength of the signal because of a long run a scheme like the one used in the radio frequency distribution system is valuable.

The detecting circuit may be coupled with the receiving antenna circuit (1) conductively, (2) inductively, and (3) capacitively. Inductive coupling is most commonly used. Conductive coupling results in low selectivity and is seldom used. Capacity coupling gives good audibility or sensitivity but poor selectivity.

Every antenna system should be provided with a lightning arrestor which will meet the requirements of the National Board of Fire Underwriters.

ELECTRIC POWER SUPPLY

Many of the modern radio sets are operated by power from the ordinary lighting circuit. The outfits used in connection with this work are known as power packs. The power packs are made to be used with either direct current or alternating current, usually at 105 to 125 volt levels. The alternating current equipment will operate on either 50 to 60 cycles or 20 to 40 cycles power supply. Where direct current is supplied to the lighting circuits it is customary to use a motor generator or a converter to get the power necessary for the receivers and amplifiers. Motor generators are used also in places where there is a low voltage lighting supply. The lighting circuit power supply is very popular now because of its convenience. Power pack equipment should be constructed to conform to all of the requirements of the National Board of Fire Underwriters, because the power output in some instances is sufficient to be dangerous to the operator as well as destructive to equipment being supplied with the power.

In spite of the rapid development made in the equipment for supplying power from an ordinary lighting circuit some makers of the best sets insist that storage batteries are necessary for certain types of service. When storage batteries are used care should be taken that they have sufficient capacity and that adequate provision is made for charging. In some instances the storage batteries are constantly kept on charge by an arrangement known as trickle charging. Unless this process is very smooth, a disturbing effect will result, especially if the storage battery power is used in the part of the equipment which receives the signals before they are amplified. In this case any disturbances will be magnified along with the signal. For charging batteries from an alternating current source bulb chargers like Tungars and Rectigons are being used by most of the best manufacturers. There are some very good copper sulphate and copper oxide rectifiers on the market which seem to have possibilities as parts of the charging equipment. In fact, they are already being used to some extent. For direct-current charging the power may be taken directly from the line for light loads or from a motor-generator set for heavy loads.

Where storage cells are used the lead sulphuric acid cells are favored because of the large power output per unit and because they are cheaper than the nickle-iron (alkaline) cells. Some makers prefer the nickle-iron cells because they will stand a large amount of abuse. Wet primary cells have hardly any use in radio equipment while dry primary cells are used in certain cases where only small capacities are needed.

VACUUM TUBES

The developments in radio equipment of nearly every kind are closely associated with the developments made in vacuum tubes. A discussion of the operating characteristics of different types of vacuum tubes would of necessity be so technical that it would be out of place in a treatment of this kind. The following are some vacuum tube production tests listed by Van Dyck and Engel: [24]

1. Appearance and mechanical conditions.
2. Condition of solder on contact pins.
3. Eccentricity of the tube bulb with respect to the base.
4. Mechanical sturdiness (bump test).
5. Initial electrical characteristics.
In order to determine the initial electrical characteristics, tests are made to obtain: 1. The filament current at rated voltage. 2. Plate current. 3. Amplification factor. 4. Plate resistance. 5. Mutual conductance. 6. Electron emission. 7. Inter-element (stem) leakage. 8. Gas content (degrees of vacuum). 9. Input impedance. 10. Grid emission. 11. Back emission. 12. Alternating current test for over-all amplification. 13. Inter-electrode capacitance. 14. Receiving set performance.

[24] Van Dyck, A. F. and Engel, F. H. "Vacuum Tube Production Tests." *Proceedings, Institute of Radio Engineers*, Vol. 16 (November 1928), No. 11, pp. 1532-52.

The demand for a large output volume from the amplifier has brought power tubes into prominence. Loud speakers have a certain sensitivity and require a definite amount of power to operate them with full volume of sound. This power must come from the output tubes, which, therefore, must be capable of delivering such power without distortion. A new type of power tube which was brought on the market this year will probably influence the character of radio equipment produced within the next few years.

The properties of individual vacuum tubes are so hard to determine that the layman will have to depend largely upon the reputation of reliable manufacturers. There are however, a few things which can be done to insure the most efficient operation of the equipment. New tubes should not be used with old tubes in the same type of service, because old tubes usually require a higher filament and plate voltage than new tubes for the same operating characteristics. Consequently, the new tubes will have an abnormally short life. The same trouble may arise if tubes of different makes are worked together. The operating characteristics of a tube change so much with age that it is well to test all tubes after a reasonable period of service to determine whether there has been any appreciable deterioration. With average usage the tubes will give excellent results for about a year.

Summary of Important Considerations

The following is a summary of the important considerations in the choice and installation of the larger units of an audio frequency distribution system. The statements given below were reviewed by ten experts before they were placed in final form.

Loud Speakers

1. *Volume (Loudness).*

The speaker shall be capable of handling all the volume necessary in the type of installation for which it was designed. It shall handle its maximum volume without appreciable distortion.

2. *Volume Control.*

Provision shall be made to vary the volume output from maximum to minimum without material loss in quality of reproduction.

3. *Simplicity.*

Consistent with sound construction, it shall have a minimum of parts to adjust or to go wrong.

4. *Rugged Construction.*

The mechanism shall be sufficiently rugged to withstand all ordinary use.

5. *"Hum" Eliminated.*

When battery eliminators are used, the 60- and 120-cycle hums produced by the alternating current power supply for the magnetic field coils of the moving coil type loud speaker shall be eliminated in such a way as to produce a minimum effect upon signals of the hum frequencies.

6. *Attractive Design.*

The over-all design shall be such that the unit will harmonize with the other furnishings of the room.

7. *Elimination of Distortion Resulting from Very High Frequencies.*

Electrical filters shall be used when necessary to remove distortion produced by high frequency harmonics and summation tones which often produce a sound that resembles a paper rattle. This does not mean that music is to be reproduced without due regard for overtones, harmonics and fine shadings.

8. *No "Barrel Effect."*

The response from the unit shall have at low frequencies, no resonant peaks which cause a booming (barrel effect) sound and continual loudness of certain low notes within a limited musical range.

9. *Ample Baffle.*

An open cone type speaker shall employ a baffle of correct characteristics for the frequency range to be reproduced. The baffle shall be sufficiently large to take care of low tones; it shall be made of reasonably thick material, and shall contain no loose parts.

10. *Paper Rattle Conditions Eliminated or Defined.*

The cone speakers shall be so constructed that they will operate within certain frequencies and volume limits without rattling.

(Manufacturers should state the maximum power in watts or AC volt-amperes which their speaker will stand without rattling.)

11. *Broad Frequency Range.*

The frequency range shall be sufficient to cover all frequencies ordinarily encountered in speech and music. A reasonable minimum requirement is 75 or 100 to 4,500 cycles (narrow ranges like 400 to 2,500 give metallic quality).

12. *Reasonably Smooth Frequency-Response Curve.*

The response curve shall not show any large peaks, especially at high and low frequency ends; on the other hand, it shall not show any marked dropping off at these extremes.

13. *Low Low-Frequency Cut-Off.*

The low frequency cut-off shall be low enough to give the reproduction ample fullness and body. This does not mean that the low frequencies shall be exaggerated. In a good dynamic loud speaker this cut-off should be at approximately 100 cycles or lower.

14. *High High-Frequency Cut-Off.*

The high-frequency cut-off shall be high enough to give brilliance and distinctness to the reproductions and to bring out the sibilants in speech. No good loud speaker should have this cut-off below 4,500 cycles.

15. *Absence of Nasal Quality.*

The response curve shall not show a distinct rise from 500 to 2,500 cycles since this is characteristic of a loud speaker which gives nasal quality.

16. *Balance Between Low- and High-Frequency Response.*

When the frequency response curve is plotted on logarithmic paper the tonal frequency responses above and below 1,000 cycles should balance.

17. *Nonresonant Material in Horns.*

The material in the horn shall be nonresonant in order that a resonant note, the frequency of which depends upon the length of the horn, shall not be produced.

18. *Size of the Horn Opening.*

The opening of the horn shall be sufficiently large to give good spread to the sound emitted.

19. *Cross Section of the Horn.*

The cross section of the horn shall increase slowly and logarithmically in passing from the neck to the opening.

20. *Neck of Horn.*

The neck of the horn must be rigid.

21. *Length of Horn Properly Related to Low-Frequency Range.*

The length of the horn shall be increased as the low frequency cut-off is lowered.

22. *Free Circulation of Air in Front of and Behind Mechanism of Cone Speakers.*

Provision shall be made for air to circulate freely in front of and behind the cone type loud speakers.

23. *Reproducers Must Be Adapted to the Acoustics of the Room.*

Loud speakers shall be chosen and placed with due regard for the acoustic properties of the room in which they are to be used.

24. *Enclosing Case.*

The enclosing case shall be made of material which is non-resonant. There shall be no loose parts which can rattle.

25. *Maintain Sensitivity.*

The magnets shall be so built that the magnetic strength will not vary to any great extent with age. This applies primarily to the permanent magnets in magnetic loud speakers.

26. *Transfer Levers.*

The transfer levers in magnetic loud speakers shall be noiseless in their operation. They shall have no appreciable natural periods.

27. *Moving Parts.*

The moving parts shall be light. They shall not be subject to warping or other deformation.

28. *Brilliant High Notes.*

The loud speaker shall reproduce high notes brilliantly but not with a piercing effect.

29. *Economical.*

The loud speaker shall possess all the necessary essentials of a good unit, but shall not carry with it purely ornamental extras.

30. *Maximum Electro-Acoustic Efficiency.*

The efficiency with which electrical energy is transferred into audio or sound energy should be as great as possible.

AUDIO FREQUENCY WIRING

1. *Ample Electrical Capacity.*

All conductors shall be of such size and material that they will be able to carry the electric current required.

2. *Proper Shielding.*

The circuits shall be so shielded that there will be no cross talk or inductive effects when several channels are run in the same conduit.

3. *Mechanical Strength.*

All wire and conduit used must be sufficiently strong to withstand the mechanical stresses to which they may be subjected.

4. *Must Meet Standards of A.I.E.E. and N.B.F.U.*

All installations shall be made in accordance with the requirements as given in the standards of the American Institute of Electrical Engineers and those of the National Board of Fire Underwriters.

5. *Flexibility.*

The circuits shall be so arranged that a maximum variety of services can be obtained. (An individual circuit from each loud speaker to the central control board provides for maximum flexibility).

6. *Proper Distribution of Loud Speaker Load.*

The loud speaker load shall be so distributed as to make possible the most efficient operation of the system.

7. *Local Rules and Regulations.*

Local requirements shall be adhered to rigidly.

8. *Easy Testing and Servicing.*

The circuits shall be so arranged that they can be tested and serviced easily.

9. *Extensions of Service.*

Provisions shall be made for future additions to the system at a minimum cost.

Central Rack and Panels

1. *Service Provisions.*

Adequate provisions shall be made for all necessary meters, control equipment, fuses, etc.

2. *Ruggedness.*

The equipment must be of substantial construction. Weak and flimsy parts shall be eliminated from places where they may affect the ruggedness of the outfit as a whole.

3. *Extensions and Additions.*

Provisions shall be made for future extensions and additions.

4. *Compactness.*

The racks and panels shall be designed to occupy the minimum possible space consistent with good construction.

5. *Operation.*

The arrangement and design of the equipment shall be such that it will not be necessary to have a highly trained technician to operate it.

6. *Economy.*

Provision shall be made for all necessary equipment but not for ornaments and useless decorations.

7. *Accessibility for Servicing.*

Sufficient space shall be left in the rear to permit easy servicing.

8. *Protective Coverings.*

Coverings shall be provided to protect the equipment from mechanical injury, accumulations of dust and interference between parts; likewise to prevent tampering and danger of contact with live parts.

9. *Standardized Construction.*

Central racks and panels shall be constructed to meet all of the requirements of the American Institute of Electrical Engineers and those of the National Board of Fire Underwriters.

10. *Stability.*

The central rack shall be so designed and installed that it cannot upset. For permanent installations the framework shall be bolted to the floor.

11. *Ease of Operation and Maintenance.*

The arrangement of the equipment on the panels and racks shall facilitate operation and maintenance.

12. *Illumination.*

Sufficient artificial and natural illumination shall be provided.

13. *Marking.*

All essential parts shall be clearly marked in order to avoid confusion on the part of the operator when handling the equipment. A complete wiring diagram and operating instructions shall be kept near the outfit.

14. *Grounding.*

The steel frames of the central racks shall be grounded.

15. *Frames.*

All equipment shall be mounted on structural steel frames to minimize fire hazards.

AUDIO FREQUENCY TRANSFORMERS

1. *Efficiency.*

High efficiency is essential to prevent loss of energy in the plate circuit. This is especially important for the output transformer.

2. *Minimum Core Loss.*

This requires a properly insulated laminated core of ample cross section.

3. *Low Self Capacity.*

This prevents short circuiting at higher frequencies. The coils are often wound in sections to make the between-layer voltage low.

4. *Low Leakage Inductances.*

This is necessary to prevent choking which causes losses at all frequencies, especially high frequencies.

5. *Good Insulation Between Windings.*

This protects the loud speaker and the operator from the high plate voltages required for power tubes. The transformer shall be tested for 1,000 volts breakdown throughout when it is to be used with tubes employing 500 volts.

6. *Capacity of Windings.*

Must be sufficient to withstand the high current values resulting from the use of power tubes.

7. *Requirements.*

Must meet the American Institute of Electrical Engineers standards and the requirements of the National Board of Fire Underwriters.

AMPLIFIERS

1. *Wave Form.*

The wave form output signal shall be practically the same as that of the input signal.

2. *Transmission and Amplification of Frequencies.*

For radio reception the amplifier and its circuits shall transmit and amplify to an equal degree all frequencies within approximately ten kilocycles of the carrier frequency.

3. *Ample Load-Carrying Capacity for the Service for Which the Unit Was Designed.*

There should be no appreciable variation in output quality for a wide variation in load.

4. *Grid Swing.*

In the audio part, the grid shall never swing appreciably positive. The grid swing shall be such that the tube will operate on the straight part of the characteristic curve.

5. *Input and Output Circuits.*

To minimize this coupling the input and the output shall be kept apart, short twisted leads in grounded metallic casing shall be used.

6. *Connections.*

All leads shall be rigidly held and all connections well soldered.

7. *Low Inaudible Frequency Mounts for Tube Sockets.*

The mounts for the tube sockets shall have such low natural frequencies that their vibrations will not produce a sound.

8. *Attachment of Parts.*

The parts of the amplifier shall be so firmly attached that there will be no rattling or moving about of these parts.

9. *Filament Power Supply.*

A steady supply of power shall be furnished for lighting the filament.

10. *Input Connections.*

Adequate provisions shall be made for connections to the input systems. These connections shall be accessible and shall facilitate making good permanent electrical contacts. Where several input systems are used, selector switches or plugs and jacks shall be furnished.

11. *Protective Coverings.*

Coverings and guards shall be furnished to protect the equipment from accumulations of dust and from mechanical injury.

12. *Marking.*

Control legends, tube position designations, etc., shall be engraved or otherwise marked in a clear and permanent manner.

13. *Over-All Dimensions.*

The over-all dimensions of the equipment shall be kept as small as possible consistent with the proper performance characteristics.

14. *Materials of Construction.*

Only standard materials of construction shall be used.

15. *Shielding.*

Shielding shall be provided in every place where there is any possibility of troublesome electrical or magnetic coupling, or acoustic howl.

16. *Substantial Construction.*

The amplifiers shall be so constructed that they will withstand all the mechanical abuse to which they may be subjected under service conditions.

17. *Simple to Operate.*

Amplifiers shall be so designed that persons not highly trained or conversant with the details of the circuits used may be able to operate the units satisfactorily.

TRANSMITTERS (MICROPHONES)

1. *Proportionality.*

The proportionality between secondary voltage of the transformer and the amplitude of the sound waves shall hold good over large variations in sound intensities.

2. *Reproduction Characteristics.*

A given sound pressure shall produce a given secondary voltage independent of frequency.

3. *Constancy of Sensitivity.*

Absolute constancy cannot be maintained; however, the transmitter shall be reasonably constant in its operation, regardless of weather conditions, etc.

4. *Critical Damping of Moving Parts.*

This is to prevent mechanical resonance which tends to accentuate some frequencies more than others.

5. *Sturdiness.*

The transmitter should be sufficiently sturdy to withstand ordinary usage.

6. *Shielding from Extraneous Noises.*

For close talking the transmitter shall be so constructed as to cut off sounds from other than the desired directions.

7. *Mounting.*

Provisions shall be made in mounting to reduce to a minimum mechanical vibrations transmitted through supports and suspensions.

PHONOGRAPH PICKUP

1. *Approximating Equal Apparent Volumes at All Musical Frequencies.*

The reproduction shall be such that all the tones within the musical scale will be reproduced with approximately equal volume as interpreted by the human ear. The musical scale is to be considered as extending from C two octaves below middle C (frequency 256 cycles per second) to C four octaves above middle C. It is not necessary for the phonograph pickup to reproduce frequencies beyond the range of the loud speaker with which it is to be used.

2. *Minimum Wear on the Record.*

The movable part of the pickup which holds the needle or stylus shall be sufficiently free in movement to permit the needle to follow the record grooves (tracings) with a minimum wear on the record. This characteristic is often referred to as armature flexibility because in most phonograph pickups the movable part is the armature. The pressure on the record shall not be heavier than is necessary for good reproduction.

3. *Construction.*

The mechanism shall be of sufficiently rugged construction to withstand ordinary usage.

4. *Volume Control.*

The volume control shall be such that the loudness can be varied from maximum to minimum output in steps which are not noticeable. Changes in volume should not cause distortion.

5. *Scratch or Surface Noise Filter.*

The over-all frequency characteristics of the pickup and the amplifying system shall be such that record scratch or surface noise will be at a minimum without sacrificing too much the frequency range near the scratch frequency.

6. *Motor Drive for the Turntable.*

The turntable shall be driven by a motor which operates on the available lighting circuit power. Where no kinds of lighting power are available the spring-driven motor shall be used.

7. *Noncorrosive Materials of Construction.*

The materials used in the construction of phonograph pickup shall be noncorrosive to the degree that they will not be affected by ordinary atmospheric conditions.

8. *Minimum Distortion.*

The mechanism shall be capable of reproducing fully from the standpoint of quality all the tones recorded on a record. The reproduced tones shall be faithful to the originals which they are to reproduce. There shall be no sluggishness in the action of any of the parts which might affect the final tone produced.

9. *Motor Speed Control.*

The motor speed control shall operate so that no change in motor speed will be sufficient to cause a discernible change in the pitch of the sound. The desirable speed regulation shall be two-tenths of one per cent, and the maximum shall be five-tenths of one per cent.

Radio Receiver

1. *Selectivity.*

The selectivity shall be such that programs can be received from desired stations without interference from other stations. (Too high selectivity is not desirable because of reduction in quality.)

2. *Sensitivity.*

The receiver shall be capable of bringing in signals with satisfactory strength and quality from broadcasting stations within the desired receiving distances. (The desired receiving distances must be reasonable.)

3. *Fidelity.*

When combined with a suitable reproducer the output tones shall be faithful reproductions of the input tones in so far as this can be controlled at a receiving station.

4. *Radio Frequency Range.*

The receiver shall operate satisfactorily at all frequencies within the broadcast range. A complete outfit shall include circuits suitable for both the ordinary broadcast reception and for short wave reception. This does not mean that the same circuits are to be used for both long and short wave reception. It might be better to have a separate short wave receiver. The change over from long wave reception to short wave reception and vice versa shall be as simple as possible.

5. *Volume.*

The receiver shall be able to produce ample volume without distortion of the service in which it is to be used.

6. *Side Band Cutting.*

The top of the response curve for the receiver shall be sufficiently broad to permit substantially equal amplification of all audio frequencies without distortion.

7. *Shielding.*

The circuits shall be shielded adequately to prevent interference between the parts and from outside sources.

8. *Simplicity of Operation.*

The number of variable controls shall be reduced to a minimum. The receiver shall be so designed that a person not highly trained or conversant with the details of the circuits used may still be able to operate the set satisfactorily.

9. *Volume Control.*

The volume control shall be capable of changing the volume smoothly.

10. *Construction.*

The chassis shall be solidly and rigidly constructed and all parts shall be fixed firmly in place. The set shall remain in serviceable condition in spite of rough handling which may be received during shipping or use.

11. *Marking of Station Selector.*

The station selector shall be so marked and illuminated that settings can be made quickly and accurately. Dials calibrated for wave lengths or frequencies are desirable.

12. *Off and On Indicator.*

There shall be some visible indicator of whether the set is off or on. This may be the same light which illuminates the station selector.

13. *Economy of Construction.*

The set shall be built primarily for service and not for ornamentation. This does not mean that the unit shall be unattractive.

14. *Stability.*

The tendency toward self-oscillation of one or more tubes shall be reduced to a minimum.

15. *Audio Frequency Amplification.*

The unit shall be able to amplify all audio frequencies within a reasonable range, say 60 to 5,000 cycles, without much variation from the average.

16. *Materials.*

All materials used shall meet the standards set up by such organizations as the American Society for Testing Materials, American Society of Mechanical Engineers, American Institute of Electrical Engineers, Radio Manufacturing Association, Electric Power Club, and American Specification Institute.

The Antenna and Lead-in Equipment

1. *Length.*

The effective length of the antenna system including the height and horizontal parts of the L type shall be such that reasonable signal strength will be obtained for those signals having frequencies within the broadcast range.

2. *Height.*

The horizontal part of an outside antenna shall be sufficiently high to clear effectively all conducting objects such as structural steel, metal roofs, trees, and guys.

3. *Ratio of Signal Strength to Disturbing Noises.*

This shall be the maximum.

4. *Strength of Parts.*

The strength of the supports, guys, and conducting wires shall be ample to withstand all ordinary usage.

5. *Insulation.*

Insulators of proper voltage rating shall be installed at all places where electrical leakage is likely to take place.

6. *Lightning Arrestor.*

The system shall be provided with a lightning arrestor which meets the requirements of the National Board of Fire Underwriters.

7. *Electrical Conductivity.*

The wire which makes up the antenna and the lead-in shall have high electrical conductivity at high frequencies.

8. *Connections.*

All connections shall be perfect from the standpoint of both mechanical strength and electrical conductivity.

ELECTRIC POWER SUPPLY

1. *Capacity.*

The power supply shall have sufficient capacity to operate the equipment satisfactorily for as long periods as the demands of the service may require.

2. *Steadiness.*

Provisions shall be made for filtering fluctuations in the power supply.

3. *Safety.*

Adequate provisions shall be made to protect the operator from dangerous shocks and burns, as well as to protect the radio equipment from damage.

4. *Simplicity.*

Any devices used in connection with the power supply shall be so simple that an untrained operator can use them correctly.

5. *Standards.*

The equipment shall meet all the standards laid down by the National Board of Fire Underwriters.

VACUUM TUBES

1. *Stability of Operation.*

The tube shall not be subject to abrupt changes in its operating characteristics while in normal service.

2. *Durability.*

All tubes shall give good service for a reasonable length of time. For ordinary radio vacuum tubes a reasonable average life is 1,000 hours of actual use.

3. *Electrical Characteristics.*

The electrical characteristics shall be such that the tube will be well adapted to the service in which it is used.

4. *Condition of Solder on Contact Pins.*

The solder on the contact pins shall have a smooth clean surface and shall cover completely the parts where contact is made.

5. *Mechanical Condition.*

There shall be no loose or weak parts in the tube which might shorten the life of the tube unduly in ordinary service.

6. *Design.*

Tubes shall be of standard design so that they can be used in ordinary equipment.

7. *Noiseless.*

Tubes operated in the circuits for which they were designed shall not set up disturbing noises.

PART II

ELECTRIC POWER SUPPLY
FOR HIGH SCHOOL SCIENCE ROOMS

INTRODUCTION

The aim of this section is to point out the power supply needs in the science rooms of a high school and to suggest ways of meeting these needs. The science rooms referred to here are those in which physics, chemistry, biology, and general science are taught. Special emphasis is placed upon physics because this science has greater electric power requirements than any other high school science. Suggested installations for the electric power supply to physics rooms are presented in Appendix B.

In the report of the Commission on Science Instruction [1] the general aims and purposes of science teaching are stated; first, with reference to the main objectives of education; second, with reference to the specific knowledge, habits, powers, interests, and ideals which should be developed. Of the seven commonly thought of objectives of education [2] upon which the work of the secondary school should be focused, the science commission believes that science instruction is especially valuable in the realization of six; namely, health, worthy home membership, vocation, citizenship, the worthier use of leisure, and ethical character. The specific values of science study as given by the science commission are: (1) the development of interests, habits, and abilities, (2) teaching useful methods of solving science problems, (3) stimulation, (4) information values, and (5) cultural and æsthetic values. The electrical power supply for the science laboratories should be such as will give the maximum aid to the realization of these objectives and values.

LECTURE DEMONSTRATION AND THE LABORATORY METHOD OF INSTRUCTION

Before arrangements are made for laboratory facilities it is necessary for those in charge to decide whether the subjects are

[1] *Reorganization of Science in Secondary Schools.* Bulletin 1920, No. 26, pp. 12-15. U. S. Bureau of Education.

[2] *Cardinal Principles of Secondary Education.* Bulletin 1918, No. 35. U. S. Bureau of Education.

to be taught by the lecture demonstration method, by the laboratory method, or by a combination of the two. The equipment requirement will depend upon the method chosen. Investigations show that each method has its advantages, depending upon the outcome desired. Downing [3] and his students have shown that for some outcomes the lecture demonstration method will give as good results as the laboratory method. Horton [4] showed that the laboratory method of instruction would give superior results where the desired outcomes involve manipulation of apparatus, and ability to solve problems in the laboratory. The kinds of results to be striven for therefore become a matter of choice on the part of those in charge of the courses to be offered. The power supply and distribution required under the two conditions are widely different. If the teacher does practically all of the work with apparatus then an elaborately equipped lecture table is all that is needed. On the other hand, if the pupils are to work with the apparatus then ample provision must be made for distribution of electric power to places where it will be most convenient for the pupil's use. Powers [5] in consideration of the studies referred to above, and others, says, "Two conclusions may be safely drawn from these studies. First, there must be larger provision for demonstrations, and second the equipment for individual work must allow for greater flexibility in the methods of teaching."

[3] Downing, Elliot R. *Teaching Science in the Schools*, pp. 111-43. University of Chicago Press, Chicago, 1925.

[4] Horton, R. E. *Measurable Outcomes from Laboratory Instruction*. Contributions to Education, No. 303. Bureau of Publications, Teachers College, Columbia University, New York, 1928.

[5] Powers, S. R. "The Selection and Purchase of Equipment and Furnishings for Laboratories." *The American School and University,* Second Annual Edition. American School Publishing Corporation, New York, 1929.

CHAPTER IV

ELECTRIC POWER SUPPLY FOR PHYSICS ROOMS

Physics in the High School Program of Studies

In planning the power supply for a laboratory it is necessary to have some idea of the demand that there will be for the subject to be taught in this laboratory. The probable future trends as to content are also important. Table II indicates that in 22 of the 30 high schools from which replies to questionnaires were received, physics is an elective subject. Moreover, 20 of the 30 physics teachers who replied believed that physics would be an elective in the future. Only 18 of the 30 thought that there was any likelihood of an advanced course in physics being given in the future. In practically all the cases where negative replies were received relative to physics being an elective subject, the teachers were working where technical courses were given considerable emphasis. Considering the results as a whole it appears that physics is now, and will probably be in the future, an elective subject in most schools except those in which technical subjects are emphasized. This conclusion is in accord with the tendency in modern education to give a great deal of freedom to the pupil in the matter of choice of subjects, and also with recommendations of the Committee on Science of the Commission on the Reorganization of Secondary Schools.[1] The constants recommended by this committee are general science and general biology. In spite of the fact that physics is not a required subject, Hunter[2] found that the percentage of schools offering physics in 1923 was slightly greater than that in 1908.

To get an idea of the shift in emphasis on that physics subject matter requiring the use of electrical power, the following questions were asked of the same 30 physics teachers:

[1] *Reorganization of Science in Secondary Schools*, Bulletin 1920, No. 26, pp. 12-15. U. S. Bureau of Education.

[2] Hunter, George W. "The Place of Science in the Secondary School." *School Review*, Vol. XXXIII (May-June 1925), pp. 370-81; 453-66.

1. Do you believe the high school physics of the future will place more emphasis on (*a*) radio or (*b*) electricity of the automobile and the aëroplane?
2. What other electrical fields do you expect to be emphasized?

Of the nineteen who expressed themselves with regard to the first question, six said that radio would be given more emphasis, and seventeen said that electricity of the automobile and the aëroplane would receive greater emphasis in the future than at present. In reply to the second question the following fields of study were suggested by various teachers: home appliances, projection apparatus, street cars, modern physics, radioactive elements, power of the atom, small motors, power generation and transmission, photo-electric cell, alternating current machinery, and vacuum tubes. Three of the teachers believed that the major emphasis would remain upon fundamental principles. These answers indicate that such electrical power should be supplied as will enable the pupil to study those topics in physics which contribute to his understanding, appreciation, and control of the everyday environment.

Courses of study offer another means for checking the trends in any subject. The writer examined those courses of study which were available at the Bureau of Curriculum Research, Teachers College. Those available were: one for the secondary schools of Indiana,[3] and the other for the Los Angeles city high schools.[4] Topics which are suggested in these courses of study, especially those parts for enrichment, strongly emphasize the study of applications of physics to real life situations. Suggestions are made to study real machines not toys.

Somewhat the same tendencies are shown in the subject matter content of the new high school physics textbooks. In four recent and widely used textbooks [5] there is much evidence in the form

[3] Wisehart, R. P. *Tentative Course of Study in Physics for the Secondary Schools of Indiana.* Bulletin 100 E-5, 1928. State Department of Public Instruction.

[4] *Course of Study Monograph, No. 34*, School Publication No. 98, Los Angeles City High Schools (June 1924).

[5] Black, N. H., and Davis, H. N. *New Practical Physics.* The Macmillan Company, New York, 1929.

Dull, C. E. *Modern Physics.* Henry Holt and Company, New York, 1929.

Fuller, R. W., Brownlee, R. B., and Baker, D. L. *Elementary Principles of Physics.* Allyn and Bacon, New York, 1927.

Millikan, R. A., Gale, H. G., Pyle, W. R. *Elements of Physics.* Ginn and Company, New York, 1927.

TABLE 2
Some Important Considerations Which Influence the Choice of Physics Laboratory Equipment

Question Number	Question	Answer	
		Yes	No
1	Is physics now a required subject in your school?	22	8
2	Do you believe physics will be an elective in the future?	20	7
3	Do you believe an advanced course in physics will be offered in the comprehensive senior high school within the next ten years?	18	9
4	Do you believe that for most of the low voltage DC work dry cells or other primary cells, or dry rectifiers like those used for radio, would be entirely satisfactory?	18	12
5	Do you run several different experiments at a time, thereby reducing the demand for electric power?	14	14
6	Do you believe that it would be as satisfactory to have the electrical outlets on the wall around the room above shelves of table height as to have them on tables as usually arranged in the room? The tables are to be movable so that they can be placed near the wall outlet when necessary.	9	15
7	Do you believe that dry wet primary batteries (like the Waterbury Telecell) might be profitably used in the laboratory in the place of dry cells or storage cells?	8	9
8	Would you favor having a small motor-generator set mounted on a truck so that it can be moved about the room thus eliminating some of the permanent wiring to individual tables?	6	24
9	In your work, except for a few portables, could the storage cells be omitted?	21	7
10	Which method of charging would you prefer— (a) Motor generator? (b) Bulb rectifier and transformer?	15 6	
11	If only portable cells are used, which would you choose— (a) Lead cells? (b) Iron nickel?	9 18	

of topics treated, illustrations used, and demonstrations suggested which supports the contention that a conscious effort is being made to have the physics student think in terms of real life situations.

These tendencies to use practical situations as much as possible have doubtless had an important part in producing the great difference between the electric power supply desired by those teachers from whom replies to a questionnaire were received and the power supply actually needed to carry out the work included in laboratory manuals, textbooks, and courses of study for physics. The actual electric power requirements based on the study of subject matter taught are given in appropriate places in the following paragraphs along with other bases for determining the proper kind of power supply.

If the work in physics is to keep pace with the very rapid developments in the field of electricity, an increasing amount of emphasis must be placed upon topics which involve the use of electric power. Physics teachers should have available not the minimum power supply necessary to carry on the work as given in textbooks, laboratory manuals, etc., but considerably more than is needed to meet these requirements in order to allow for enrichment of the subject matter offered.

LABORATORY PRACTICE

The number of pupil stations to which electric power must be supplied depends upon at least two important factors; namely, the number of pupils who work together, and the percentage of time in the school day during which the laboratory is in use. The second column of Table 3 indicates that in those schools from which replies were obtained, it is generally customary to have two pupils work together on an average experiment. No replies indicated that there were more than four pupils in a group. These practices agree with those which the writer observed in the high schools he visited and also with those common in the laboratories for the first course in college physics which in many respects have much in common with a good high school course. If past practices can be taken as a guide then provision will need to be made for not more than half as many pupil station electric power outlets as there are pupils in the class. Where provisions can be made to have someone in charge of the laboratory throughout the day, the required number of pupil stations can be reduced by having sections of a class occupy the laboratory at different times. This arrangement is practical only when the room is not used to capacity. The third column of Table 3 shows that the laboratories were used every period of the day in only six of the thirty schools from which reports were obtained. In one school the laboratory was used only 16 per cent of the time.

TABLE 3

PUPIL USE OF THE LABORATORY

Replies to Questionnaire

SCHOOL NUMBER*	NUMBER OF PUPILS WORKING TOGETHER ON AN AVERAGE EXPERIMENT	PERCENTAGE OF THE AVAILABLE TIME FOR WORK THAT THE PHYSICS LABORATORY IS IN USE
1	2	70
2	2	80
3	2	100
4	2	37
5	3 or 4	50
6	2	75
7	2—4	50—100
8	2	69
9	4	50
10	2	100
11	2	100
12	2—4	90
13	2	40
14	3	90
15	2	50
16	2	40
17	2	70
18	2 or 3	40
19	4	47
20	2	100
21	2	67
22	2	57
23	1 or 2	60
24	2	100
25	2	50
30	2	33
31	4	86
32	2	25
33	2	16
34	2	100

* Each school from which a reply was obtained was given a number, the designating number for each school remaining the same in all of the tables in Part II of this study.

The median percentage for the group is 68. Morphet [6] found the following medians for room utilization of physics laboratories on the basis of class periods: (1) in those schools with enrollments of over 1,000 the average was 77.7 per cent; (2) in those with enrollments between 500 and 1,000 the average was 47 per cent; and (3) in those having enrollments less than 500 the average was 54.4 per cent. It seems probable, therefore, that the number of pupil stations might be reduced in many cases if the laboratories were used all the time.

If it is impossible to arrange the classes so that the physics laboratory can be used all the time for physics laboratory purposes, then it is advisable to equip the room so that it can be used for other laboratory work or for classroom work. Fixed tables of the kind usually found in physics laboratories are not well adapted to use in rooms where class work is carried on in an informal way. If the outlets for gas and electricity are located along the walls around the room, there is no need for large fixed tables. Moreover, the room could be changed from a laboratory to a regular classroom without tearing up floors and removing pipes. In order to get the viewpoint of physics teachers regarding this arrangement the following question was asked: "Do you believe that it would be as satisfactory to have the electrical outlets on the walls around the room above shelves of table height as to have them on tables arranged in the room? The tables are to be movable so that they can be placed near the wall outlet when necessary." Question 6 in Table 2 gives a summary of the positive and negative answers. Only nine teachers favored the arrangement without reservation, and fifteen definitely objected to it. Of the six remaining returns, four favored having wall outlets in addition to the table outlets and two expressed no opinion. According to Professor N. H. Black of Harvard University [7] portable tables and wall outlets are used in some of the schools in Europe. Professor Black observed also the use of portable motor generators in some of the European schools. With a portable motor-generator set and a small attached panelboard mounted on a truck, it would be possible to supply pupil stations with power without much permanent piping. This would

[6] Morphet, E. L. *The Measurement and Interpretation of School Building Utilization.* Contributions to Education, No. 264, Bureau of Publications, Teachers College, Columbia University, New York, 1927.

[7] Personal interview.

minimize the need for fixed tables. The answers to Question 8 in Table 2 indicate that most of these physics teachers did not favor the use of a motor-generator set in this way. In fact, only six of the thirty answered in the affirmative. Mr. L. W. Lyon, head assistant in physics, Soldan High School, St. Louis, strongly favors the portable motor generators. He recommends the use of 200 to 700 watt outfits. In spite of the fact that the writer has not seen either the wall outlets or the portable motor-generator sets in use in the high schools visited, he is of the opinion that both arrangements are worthy of serious consideration for use in the modern high school. These arrangements would offer great flexibility in services afforded and economy of installations required.

POWER REQUIREMENTS FOR THE LABORATORY

In order to arrive at the power requirements in the physics laboratories the writer used the following methods of investigation: (1) questionnaires to twenty-two physics teachers and interviews with others; (2) study of content of courses of study, laboratory manuals, and textbooks; (3) examination of recommended and required lists of equipment; (4) study of plans and specifications; (5) interviews; and (6) visits to the various schools.

The Number of Experiments Requiring Electricity.

The second column of Table 4 indicates that the number of experiments given by the different teachers who replied to the questionnaire varies greatly. The number ranges from 7 to 50 with a median of about 13. To arrive at the median the writer used the average for each case in which two numbers were given.

The data in the third column of Table 4 indicate a wide variation in the number of experiments given which require more than six volts DC. The most common number is 3 and the offerings in most of the schools would be covered by 5 or fewer experiments of this type. From the data given in the fourth column it will be seen that two experiments requiring 2 amperes or more at 6 volts or less DC is as many as most of these teachers offer. The fifth column of Table 4 shows that offerings in most of the schools can be met with three or fewer experiments which require more than 24 volts DC. The data in this table suggest the possibility of diminishing the laboratory requirements for electric power by arranging properly the schedule of experiments. The summary of replies to Question 5 in Table 2 indicates that half these teachers are reducing the power load by running several different experiments at the same time.

TABLE 4

NUMBER OF EXPERIMENTS IN FIRST COURSE IN PHYSICS REQUIRING
ELECTRICITY

Replies to Questionnaire

SCHOOL NUMBER	TOTAL NUMBER OF EXPERIMENTS REQUIRING ELECTRICITY	THE NUMBER OF EXPERIMENTS REQUIRING		
		More Than 6 Volts DC	Two or More Amperes at 6 Volts or Less	More Than 24 Volts DC
1	14	1	1	0
2	36	6	2	4
3	20	Many	0	Many
4	8	0	2	0
5	14	3	3	3
6	12	2	4	2
7	10	Few	Few	
8	13	8	2	12
9	20	0	0	0
10	15	6	?	5
11	6	0	0	2
12	15—50	80%	Few	80%
13	25	?	11	2
14	15	5	2	2
15	15	6	2	6
16	10	3	7	3
17	10	3	0	3
18	10	5	4	5
19	16	8	0	8
20	12—15	5	4	4
21	18	3		3
22	12	5	4	5
23	10—15	5—6	1	6
24	7	0		
25	14	8	4	8
30	18	8	6	3
31	12	3		Few
32	12	3		1
33	10	3	2	0
34	18	3		3—4

A study of six widely used physics laboratory manuals [8]
showed that approximately one-fifth of the experiments given
require the use of electricity. The average for the number of
these experiments listed in the manuals is approximately the
same as that obtained above from the returns from teachers in
the field; namely, thirteen or fourteen. None of the experiments
listed absolutely require 2 amperes or more at 6 volts or less.
While some of the experiments can be performed with the use
of DC at levels above 6 volts, these higher voltages are not
needed if a 110 volt source of AC is available. Many teachers
use laboratory directions which they have prepared themselves.
These laboratory directions are written to suit the power supply
available. Special interests of the teachers or the students may
have affected the number and kinds of experiments performed.

Alternating Current (AC) Voltages.

Table 5 gives the laboratory power requirements from the
standpoint of what the teachers are now using and what they
consider desirable. The data in the second column indicate that
AC voltages ranging from 110 to 120 are used in fourteen of
the twenty-two schools, that in four schools provisions are made
for obtaining various voltage levels from low voltages to 110, that
220 volts are used in three schools, and that six of the schools
have no provision for AC. The second column shows that four
of the six teachers who do not have AC available believe that
it is desirable. Three of them wish to have it at several voltage
levels between 0 and 110. Four of the teachers who now have
AC did not state definitely that they believed that this power
was desirable. These replies indicate that 110 volts AC should
be supplied to the physics laboratory, and that in some cases
220 volts AC and steps of AC supply between 0 and 110 are
desirable for the first course in physics.

[8] Black, N. H. *Laboratory Experiments in Practical Physics.* The Macmillan Company,
New York, 1927.
  Dull, C. E. *Laboratory Exercises in Physics.* Henry Holt and Company, New York,
1929.
  Fuller, R. W., Brownlee, R. B. and Baker, D. L. *Laboratory Exercises in Physics.*
Allyn and Bacon, New York, 1927.
  Good, F. F. *Laboratory Projects in Physics.* The Macmillan Company, New York,
1923.
  Millikan, R. A., Gale, H. G. and Davis, I. C. *Exercises in Laboratory Physics for
Secondary Schools.* Ginn and Company, New York, 1925.
  Sears, F. E. *Laboratory Manual of Physics.* F. M. Ambrose and Company, Boston,
1928.

TABLE 5

PHYSICS LABORATORY POWER REQUIREMENTS

Replies to Questionnaire

SCHOOL NUMBER	ALTERNATING CURRENT				DIRECT CURRENT			
	Volts		Amperes		Volts		Amperes	
	Using	Desired	Using	Desired	Using	Desired	Using	Desired
1 ..	110	110	10	20	8	110	30	30
2 ..	110		20		110		30	
3 ..	6—110							
4 ..	110	110	15	15	24	24	15	20
5 ..	0—110	0—110	0—20	0—20	0—220	0—220	0—40	0—40
7 ..	110 220	110 220	5—15	5—15	4—8		30	
8 ..	0—120	0—120	0—30	0—30	0—12 0—115	0—12 0—115		
9 ..	0	0—110	0	0—10	0—110		0—10	
10 ..	0	10—20 110—220	0	100—50 25—15	110	6—15 110	25	100—50—25
11 ..	Dry cells and current supplied by city all that is necessary or desirable							
12 ..	0—220	0—220	0—5		0—110	0—220		
13 ..					110	110	0—5	0—15
14 ..					110	6—110	House Supply	
15 ..	110	110	40	40	110	110	20	20
16 ..					110		50	
17 ..	0	110	0	10	110	110	20	20
18 ..					2—110	2—110	5—75	5—75
19 ..	110	110	20	20	12—150	12—150	0—60	0—60
20 ..	115	12—15 115	30	30	6—8 100—125	6—8 100—125	0—25	0—25
23 ..	0	110	0	50	110	32	50	50
24 ..	0	6—110	0	10—50		4—110		5—50
30 ..	110 220	110 220	0—15	0—15	2—150	2—150	10	10
31 ..	110	110 220	0—15	15	2—150	2—150	10	10
32 ..	110		0—10		32		0—30	

The fifth column of Table 6 shows the data regarding AC voltage requirements for an advanced course in physics. All the teachers (22) who gave any opinion regarding this point felt that 110 volts AC should be supplied. Nine of them believed that 220 volts AC should be furnished. AC at different voltage

TABLE 6

PROBABLE POWER REQUIREMENTS FOR AN ADVANCED COURSE IN PHYSICS

Replies to Questionnaire

School Number	Characteristics of DC Power Supplied to Laboratory		Would a Motor Generator Plus Portable Storage Cells and Dry Cells Furnish a Satisfactory DC Supply?	Characteristics of AC Supply to Laboratory		
	Volts	Amperes		Volts	Amperes	Phases
1 ..	550	20—30	?	220	10—20	1 and 3
3 ..	4—110	?	Yes	110	?	1 and 3
4 ..	110	15	No	110	15	1 and 3
5 ..	0—220	0—40	Yes	0—115	0—40	1 and 3
6 ..	50—110 4—10	50	Yes	50—110 0—25	50	1 and 3
7 ..	4—8	30	Yes	110—220	0—15	1 and 3
8 ..	0—120	0—30	Yes	0—120	0—30	1 and 3
9 ..	0—110	0—20	Yes	0—110	0—20	1
10 ..	6—15—110	110—50—25	Yes	110—220 10—20	100—50 25—15	1 and 3
11 ..			Probably			
12 ..	0—220	?	Yes	0—110—220	?	1 and 3
14 ..	110—220	50	Yes	110	50	1 and 2
15 ..	110	30	Yes	110	40	1 and 2
16 ..	110	50	Yes	220	50	2
17 ..	110	50		110	50	1, 2, 3
19 ..	220 6—8	50	Yes	220 12—15	50	1 and 3
20 ..	110—125 220—250	0—50	Yes	110—115 220—250	0—50	1, 2, 3
21 ..	220	30	Yes	110	30	1
23 ..	110	50	Yes	110	50	1 and 3
24 ..			Yes			
25 ..	5—220	5—50	Yes	110	0—50	1 and 3
30 ..	125	15	No	110—220	5—10	1, 2, 3
31 ..	150	12	Yes	110	12	1, 2, 3
32 ..	6—220	0—10	Yes	110—220	0—10	1 and 2

levels between the upper and lower limits available was considered desirable by eight of the teachers. These data indicate that the principal difference between the desirable AC voltages for the first course in physics and the advanced course lies in the greater emphasis of the 220 volt level in the latter.

From the data in the second column of Table 7 it may be seen that in 17 of the 30 schools covered, motors in the laboratory

TABLE 7

POWER REQUIREMENTS FOR DRIVING MOTORS IN THE PHYSICS DEPARTMENT

Replies to Questionnaire

SCHOOL NUMBER	MAXIMUM AMPERAGE REQUIRED AT ANY ONE TIME FOR MOTORS			
	110 Volt Level AC	220 Volt Level AC	110 Volt Level DC	6 Volt Level DC
1	35			6
2	30		30	
3	10		10	
4	20		10	15
5			20	
6	50		50	?
7	7	15	7	10
8	2—3		2	
9			10	10
10	25	15	25	50
14			30	4
15	10—15	10	10	20
16			24	16
17	20		20	20
18				72
19			20	10
20	20		30	16—18
21	2		5	
22	50		30	20
23	20	5	50	25
30	10	6	10	10
31	6		6	10
32	10		10	

are driven from the 110 AC supply. This same table shows that 220 volts AC is used for driving motors in five of the schools. The laboratory manuals and the textbooks referred to previously gave no indication of the use of motors rated higher than 110 volts. The lists of equipment assembled by the Central Scientific Company [9] do not include the pieces of apparatus which require 220 volts AC. Voltmeters with scale readings up to 300 volts are recommended in some state lists. This indicates that those who prepared the lists thought that these high voltages would be encountered in some parts of the work. Monahan [10] does not include in his list any apparatus which requires 220 volts AC.

[9] *Standard State Lists of High School Laboratory Equipment.* Central Scientific Company, Chicago, 1927. [10] Monahan, A. C. *Laboratory Layouts for the High School Sciences.* Bulletin 1927, No. 22. U. S. Bureau of Education.

Alternating Current (AC) Amperages.

In the fourth column of Table 5 it may be seen that amperages of the AC now used in the laboratories covered range from 0 to 40. The most common maximum amperage reported is 15. For approximately 77 per cent of all the cases reported as using AC, a maximum of twenty amperes would cover the requirements. This current could be carried safely by the ordinary Number 12 rubber-insulated wire used in house wiring. From the fifth column of Table 5 it may be seen that the maximum amperages desired are higher than those available, one teacher desiring 100 amperes. Here a maximum of twenty amperes would meet the requirements of 60 per cent of the teachers who reported.

The current requirements for an advanced course in physics are given in the sixth column of Table 6. These current requirements are, in general, much higher than those for the first course. In fact, the most common amperage called for is 50.

For driving AC motors used in the laboratory the requirements at the 110 volt level and 220 volt level are given in the second and third columns of Table 7. The second column indicates that twenty amperes at 110 volts will be sufficient for two-thirds of the cases reported. The maximum amperage reported for the operation of 220 volt AC motors is 15. The amperage requirements stated above are considerably above those needed for the experiments given in the standard laboratory manuals referred to on page nine. Experiments with household appliances require the largest amperage; these do not exceed five or six amperes per unit. The published standard state lists of equipment recommended for high schools give only a few items which require the use of AC.

Alternating Current (AC) Phases.

In the eighth and ninth columns of Table 8 data are given concerning the necessary and the desirable phases characteristic of the AC supplied to the laboratory for the first course in physics. Twenty of the twenty-four teachers who replied felt that only single-phase AC was necessary. Fifteen thought that it would be desirable to have three-phase AC available also. Two-phase AC was considered desirable by only four of these teachers.

The last column of Table 6 lists the phases AC which these

TABLE 8

PHASES AC WHICH SHOULD BE SUPPLIED TO THE PHYSICS PANEL BOARD

Replies to Questionnaire

SCHOOL NUMBER	PHASES NECESSARY			ADDITIONAL PHASES DESIRABLE		
	Single	Two-Phase	Three-Phase	Single	Two-Phase	Three-Phase
1	x					x
2	x					x
3	x					x
4	x					
6	x					x
7	x		x			
8			x			
9	x					
10	x					x
11	x	x				x
12	x					x
14	x					
15	x				x	
17	x				x	x
18	x					
19	x					x
20	x					
21	x					
22				x		x
23	x					
25	x					x
30	x				x	x
31	x				x	x
32	x					x
33	x	x				x

physics teachers believe should be supplied to the physics laboratory for an advanced course. Practically all of them are of the opinion that both single-phase and three-phase AC should be supplied. In only two cases is single-phase called for alone. Two-phase AC is mentioned in only eight cases.

These data reflect the tendency on the part of many teachers to have the pupils learn about and work with that which is used in actual life situations. Single-phase AC is common for lighting service while three-phase AC is common for power service. Two-phase AC is not being used as much now as it was some time ago. It is evident that if three-phase AC is not furnished from the regular power service, then the proper portable equipment should be supplied so that three-phase AC can be generated for use in demonstration work if not in laboratory work.

The study of textbooks, courses of study, laboratory manuals, and lists of equipment indicates that there is very little use for any but single-phase AC in the usual course in high school physics. On the other hand, there is a tendency to include more practical topics in the course. This probably accounts for the desire on the part of some teachers to include in their courses some study of two-phase and three-phase AC.

Direct Current (DC) Voltage.

The data in the sixth column of Table 5 indicate that most of these teachers are using DC voltages of 110 to 150 volts. Where the low voltages are indicated separately, a maximum of twelve volts includes all but two of the cases. A number of the laboratories receive their supply from generators which supply power for entire buildings. In many of these cases various voltages are obtained by the use of rheostats. In most cases the teachers are satisfied with the DC power supply which they now have. One teacher said that the power supplied by the city and that obtainable from dry cells is all that is necessary or desirable. These data show that the DC voltage requirement can be met, in general, if the high voltage source of supply ranges from 100 to 150 volts and the low voltage source will furnish as much as twelve or fifteen volts. The intermediate voltages can be obtained by the use of resistances.

The data referred to in the preceding paragraph have to do with the first course in physics. The data in the second column of Table 2 give the opinions of the same teachers regarding the DC voltage requirements for an advanced course. These data indicate that the high voltages ranging from 110 to 220 and higher should be available. One teacher believes that 550 volts should be furnished. The low voltage requirements are approximately the same as those for the first course.

The number of experiments requiring DC power at several voltage levels is given in Table 4 which was previously discussed. These results indicate that but few experiments are generally offered at the several power levels and that the current demands .can be considerably reduced by careful scheduling of experiments, particularly those requiring the low voltage levels.

The fourth and fifth columns of Table 7 show that in practically all schools the 110 volt DC is used for driving motors in the laboratory and that in more than half these schools the six volt DC is used for the same purpose. There are six schools in which only one voltage level is used.

Here again the study of laboratory manuals, courses of study, and lists of equipment shows that most of the experiments which require DC can be performed with the use of a low voltage supply. In fact, most of the laboratory directions call for from two to seven dry cells or six to twelve volt storage batteries. Most of the manuals give alternative directions which include provision for the use of the 110 volt supply. No experiments are suggested which require or supply higher than 110 volts.

Direct Current (DC) Amperage.

According to the data given in the sixth column of Table 5 the DC amperage used ranges from practically 0 to 75. If the maximum value is taken in each case where two values are given, the median amperage used is between twenty-five and thirty. If averages are considered in each case where two values are given, the median is about twenty amperes. Since several schools covered in these replies offer trade courses it is probable that twenty to twenty-five amperes DC would meet all ordinary demands in most places. The ninth column of Table 5 shows that although the desired amperage in a few cases is higher than that which is now available, a twenty-five ampere DC supply would satisfy half the teachers if only maximum values in each case were considered.

The data in the third column of Table 6 indicate that a maximum of fifty amperes DC is sufficient for an advanced course in physics. Only one teacher believed that more amperage would be necessary. The DC load in any particular place will depend upon the type of advanced course offered, and upon the manner in which the experiments are scheduled.

The DC amperage required for driving motors is given in the fourth and fifth columns of Table 7. The data in the fourth column show that twenty amperes will care for the 110 volt motor load in two-thirds of the schools from which replies were received. According to the results in the fifth column twenty amperes would be sufficient for the six volt motor load in the laboratories of 82 per cent of the schools. Here again the high amperages are required in schools where trade courses are offered.

The study of laboratory manuals and recommended lists of equipment reveals no need for high DC amperage for any of the usual high school physics experiments. The current drawn for charging storage batteries represents one of the largest drains. This rarely amounts to over six amperes at the charging voltage and therefore would be proportionately less depending upon the number of cells to be charged and the voltage of the power supply. If the electric power supply for the whole building is DC, then this source is ample for all experiments which require direct current, especially if a few dry cells or a small storage battery are available. Unless special apparatus is used, a maximum of twenty amperes at 110 volts is sufficient for all ordinary work.

Power Requirements for Lecture Demonstration

The power requirements for lecture demonstrations are influenced greatly by the attitude of the teacher with respect to the importance of this method of instruction and by his willingness to make use of the equipment which is available. It seems reasonable to believe that the power supply for demonstration purposes should be at least as extensive as that for laboratory work, particularly in the way of kinds of services available.

Alternating Current (AC) Voltage.

When the data in the second and third columns of Table 9 are compared with those in the corresponding columns of Table 5, it is apparent that these teachers are now using the same AC voltage levels for lecture demonstration work as for the laboratory work and are of the opinion that the voltage requirements in both situations are about the same. The data indicate that most of the work may be done if the regular lighting circuit voltage is available. Several teachers consider it desirable to have AC at the 220 volt level and also at ten to fifteen volts in addition to the 110 volt level which the usual lighting service furnishes.

The power requirements for the projection equipment used in connection with lectures and demonstrations must be considered. The second column of Table 10 gives the voltage levels used for

TABLE 9

Physics Lecture-Room Power Requirements

Replies to Questionnaire

School Number	Alternating Current				Direct Current			
	Volts		Amperes		Volts		Amperes	
	Using	Desired	Using	Desired	Using	Desired	Using	Desired
1 ...	110	110	10	20	8	110	30	30
2 ...	110		20		110		30	
3 ...	6—110							
4 ...	110	110	15	15	24	24	15	20
5 ...	0—110	0—110	0—20	0—20	0—220	0—220	0—40	0—40
7 ...	110 220	110 220	5—15	5—15	4—8		30	
8 ...	0—120	0—120	0—30	0—30				
9 ...		0—110		0—50	0—110		0—80	
10 ...	0	10—20 110—220	0	100—50 25—15	110	6—15 110	25	100—50—25
11 ...	Dry cells and current supplied by city all that is necessary or desirable							
12 ...	0—?		0—5	?	0—110	0—220	0—5	0—5
13 ...					110	110	0—5	0—30
15 ...	110	110	40	40	110	110	20	20
16 ...					110		50	
17 ...	0	110	0	10	110	110	20	20
18 ...	110	110	1—20	1—20	2—110	2—110	1—25	1—50
19 ...	110 115	110 12—15	20 30	20 30	12—150 6—8	12—150 6—8	0—60 0—25	0—60 0—25
20 ...		115 220—230			100—125	100—125		
23 ...	0	110	0	50	110	32	25	50
24 ...		4—110		3—50		2—110		3—50
30 ...	110 220	110 220	0—15	0—15	2—150	2—150	10	0
31 ...	110 220	110 220	0—15	15	2—150	2—150	10	10
32 ...	110		0—10		32		0—30	

slide projection and the fourth column gives those used for opaque projection. These data indicate that nearly all the projectors commonly used in these schools are designed to operate from the regular 110 volt AC or DC lighting service. Those projectors which do not operate from this service usually employ direct current arcs as the source of light. They are used when very intense illumination is necessary.

The authors of new textbooks and courses of study recognize a need for furnishing a certain amount of subject matter which deals with alternating current phenomena. While most of the illustrations given and demonstrations suggested require the 110 volt level, there are a few instances in which 10 volts and 220 volts are desirable.

Alternating Current (AC) Amperage.

The amperages reported as being used in the lecture-room are given in the fourth column of Table 9. The data show that the maximum amperage is 40 and that in approximately 80 per cent of the schools twenty amperes or less are used. The values given in the fifth column of this same table indicate that some

TABLE 10

VOLTAGE AND AMPERAGE REQUIRED FOR OPERATING PROJECTION APPARATUS
IN THE PHYSICS DEPARTMENT

Replies to Questionnaire

SCHOOL NUMBER	SLIDE PROJECTOR		OPAQUE PROJECTOR	
	Volts	Amperes	Volts	Amperes
1	110	10	110	10
2	110	30	110	30
3	110	10	110	10
4	110	10	110	10
5	110	4	110	40
7	110	10		
8	115	2—5	115	10
11	110	2	110	5
12	110	10		
13	110	5	110	50
14	110	4	110	25
15	110	15	110	15
16	110	50	110	50
17	110	10	110	10
18	110	9		
19	110	10		
20	110	4	110	10
21	110	5–10	110	30
23	110	5	110	10
24	110	10	110	.10
25	110	5	110	10
30	110	10		
31	110	5		

teachers are of the opinion that amperages as high as 50 or 100 are desirable. Slightly more than half the teachers who reported gave the desirable amperage as twenty or less. Thus it seems wise to supply at least twenty amperes AC, and preferably as much as fifty, for the lecture demonstration work. The larger amperage certainly would meet all the requirements for the demonstrations suggested in textbooks and courses of study. The twenty ampere supply would be ample for practically all demands.

The third and fifth columns of Table 10 show that where AC power is supplied to the projection apparatus 10 amperes on the service line is all that is required for each projector. In order to be safe it is advisable to wire for about twenty amperes. When higher amperages than these are used at the light source, the power is taken from the secondary of a transformer or from a direct current source.

Alternating Current (AC) Phases.

With respect to phase characteristics, as many kinds of alternating current should be supplied for lecture demonstration purposes as are supplied for laboratory use. In fact, it seems reasonable to make some provision for three-phase AC in addition to ordinary single-phase AC because the three-phase AC is used so commonly for commercial induction motors. If a commercial supply of the three-phase power is not available then it is probably advisable to use some portable source. This portable source might be in the form of an experimental piece of apparatus or a small commercial outfit. A portable source is convenient because it is adaptable for study purposes.

As stated elsewhere in this chapter, there is sufficient interest in the study of two-phase and three-phase AC, in addition to single-phase, to cause textbook and course of study authors to include subject matter to satisfy these interests.

Direct Current (DC) Voltage.

The sixth column of Table 9 shows that the DC voltages throughout the entire range from 0 to 110 are in common use. One teacher reported that he was using voltages as high as 220. In most cases where only 110 volts are supplied, the lower voltages are obtained by the use of resistances. The seventh column of the same table shows that there are no radical differences between the voltages now being used and those which the teachers consider desirable. The results indicate that the DC supply should provide for voltages from 110 or 150 down. The demonstrations suggested in textbooks and in courses of study could be conducted satisfactorily with a power supply having the voltage range suggested above. It is true that most demonstrations could be carried out with the use of low voltages only, but in order to do this the demonstrator would, in some instances, be forced to work with small demonstration equipment instead of the regular units which the student finds in use in life situations. Sometimes commercial units are of such a nature that small demonstration models are more valuable for study purposes than are the commercial units themselves.

Direct Current (DC) Amperage.

In the eighth column of Table 9 are shown the DC amperages used in physics lecture demonstration work of the schools from which reports were received. They range from zero to eighty. In fourteen of the eighteen schools the maximum amperage used for this purpose is thirty or less. The ninth column of Table 9 shows that in six of the fourteen schools the physics teachers would like to have more than thirty amperes DC available. In fact five of them desire fifty amperes or more. On the basis of these results the wiring to the lecture table should be of sufficient capacity to carry heavy currents.

If provision is made for the large amperages given above, the teacher can use projection equipment which employs the large carbon arc as the light source. In the schools which the writer visited the maximum amperage required for the carbon arcs was twenty-five.

Unless a large number of demonstrations are run at the same time, a maximum of thirty amperes would be ample for the demonstrations suggested in textbooks and courses of study which the writer reviewed. The current requirement at the 110 volt level is small; one ampere or less is approximately the normal requirement unless DC is used in connection with household appliances, in which case five or six amperes is ample. This amperage is large enough for most low voltage work. Very large amperage at low voltage is generally obtained from portable storage batteries and not over systems of permanent wiring.

Power Requirements for the Physics Shop.

Many schools do not provide a separate shop for the physics department and those schools which do have provisions of this kind usually have the same supply of electric power in the shop as in the laboratory. The facts may be seen by comparing Table 5 with Table 11. Either 110 volts AC or 110 volts DC is supplied to practically all the shops. In some cases 220 volts is desired for motor drive. The three-phase 220 volts AC is especially convenient for machines equipped with induction motors. For the shop work necessary in connection with the first course in physics, the pumps, lathes, saws, and other machines which require motors are generally designed for use with the 110 volt or 220 volt AC or the 110 volt DC supply. In fact, some machines are equipped with universal motors which operate from either an AC or a DC supply. For all small motors the regular house wiring will have sufficient current carrying capac-

TABLE 11

PHYSICS SHOP (PREPARATION ROOM) POWER REQUIREMENTS

Replies to Questionnaire

School Number	ALTERNATING CURRENT				DIRECT CURRENT			
	Volts		Amperes		Volts		Amperes	
	Using	Desired	Using	Desired	Using	Desired	Using	Desired
1	110	110	10	20	8	110	30	30
2	110		20		110		30	
3	6–110							
4	110	110	15	15	24	24	15	20
5	0–110	0–110	0–20	0–20	0–110	1–110	0–40	0–40
7	110 220	110 220	5–15	5–15	4–8		10	
8	0–120	0–120	10	10	115			
9					0–110		0–50	
10	0	10–20 100–220	0	100–50 25–15	110	6–15 110	25	100–50–25
15	110	110	40	40	110	110	20	20
20	115	115	30	30	0	0	0	0
23	0	110	0	10	220	32	25	50
24	Power 220–3 phase Pump 110–1 "			3–50		2–110		3–50

ity. If any machines are used which require much power, they should be equipped with 220 volt motors. The only other kinds of equipment which would require high amperage are the electric furnaces. Most of these can be operated satisfactorily on 110 volts 10 amperes. If higher amperages are desired it is advisable to draw the electric power from the secondary of a transformer.

In practically all the schools that the writer visited the wiring was arranged so that all the power available at the central panel board could be supplied to the electric outlets in the shop. When the panel board is so placed that the front of the board is in the laboratory and the back of it in the shop, it is not expensive to install the necessary wiring and conduit for supplying the shop with any kind of power that is available at the panel board.

PANEL BOARDS AND ALLIED EQUIPMENT

It is now a rather common practice to bring all the electrical power to a central point for distribution to the laboratories, lecture-rooms, and shops. In fact, the practice is sufficiently common to warrant electrical manufacturers' building more or less standard equipment for this purpose. Within the past year these manufacturers have designed panel boards which meet the requirements of the National Board of Fire Underwriters. From the standpoint of services offered and equipment furnished in connection with the panel boards, there is practically no limit to the elaborateness, provided the purchaser is willing to pay the price. Since there is considerable difference of opinion regarding the manner in which the electric power supply for the physics department should be distributed, the following information is furnished to show what is being done now and to point out some important considerations in planning new installations. Important considerations regarding panel board equipment and installation are given in Appendix C.

Storage Batteries and Charging Devices.

In many physics departments storage batteries are utilized as a source of low voltage DC. Some teachers use the storage cells extensively, others use them very little, if at all. Where elaborate power supply equipment is furnished the storage batteries are generally made a fixed part of this equipment.

Since interviews with physics teachers revealed a considerable difference of opinion regarding the use of storage cells, the writer sought further information regarding this point by including Questions 9, 10, and 11 of Table 2 in the questionnaire referred to in the preceding discussions of this section.

The replies to Question 9 of Table 2 show that 21 of the 28 teachers who replied believe that except for a few portables the storage cells could be omitted. The particular type of storage cell preferred by these teachers is indicated in the replies to Question 11 of Table 2. The summary shows that 18 prefer the iron-nickel type and 9 prefer the lead type. The principal reasons given for favoring the lead type are: (1) it is more useful for study purposes because the pupil can see the parts and because this type of cell is so commonly used; (2) a large capacity can be obtained from a small number of units; and (3) the initial cost of lead cells is less than that of iron-nickel cells. The reasons given for favoring the iron-nickel cells are: (1) the cells are mechanically rugged; (2) they can be left uncharged without any apparent damage; and (3) they are not damaged by short circuits. Monahan [11] favors the use of iron-nickel cells for practically the same reasons given above.

According to the summary of opinions regarding the manner of charging the storage cells, Question 10 of Table 2 shows that 15 of those who replied favor the use of a motor generator while 6 favor using a bulb charger. The motor generator has the advantage in that it can be a DC supply for experimental purposes as well as for charging the storage cells. Bulb rectifiers are not suitable for the DC supply for experimental purposes because of their limited capacity. They are cheaper than motor-generator sets and are especially well adapted to use with automatic charging devices. If the storage battery is connected with a panel board the rectifier should be permanently mounted on this board so that it is available when needed. Many of the teachers interviewed by the writer said that when the bulb chargers were not permanently mounted on the panel board they were frequently taken to other parts of the building. Carrying chargers from place to place is a bad practice for the reason stated above and also because the outfit is likely to be damaged or lost. Where the line supply is AC, devices other than the

[11] Monahan, A. C., *op. cit.*, p. 23.

bulb chargers or motor generators can be used, especially if the required charging current is low. The so-called dry plate rectifiers of the copper oxide and copper sulphide types have become popular recently. They are particularly well suited to charging at rates of fractions of an ampere. These types of rectifiers as well as the liquid electrolytic rectifiers are now commonly used when batteries are kept on continuous charge, so that energy is constantly being put into the cells to replace that which is lost as the cells stand idle. Continuous charging makes possible the use of smaller ampere hour capacity cells for a given service than are required when intermittent charging is provided. It also greatly simplifies the care of the storage batteries. In places where the line supply is DC, batteries can be charged from this source, provided the proper resistances are used. Where much current is needed and where power is supplied at considerably higher levels than the required charging voltage, much energy is lost in reducing the voltage to the proper level.

Where storage cells are connected to a panel board for distribution of power, provision should be made for obtaining voltages in steps of two volts each and multiples thereof. It should be possible also to charge any particular cell which may need it without affecting the others. The data in Table 11A show that a maximum of twelve volts is ample for the storage battery

TABLE 11A

VOLTAGE WHICH SHOULD BE OBTAINED FROM STORAGE BATTERIES

Replies to Questionnaire

SCHOOL NUMBER	VOLTAGE	SCHOOL NUMBER	VOLTAGE
1	6.6	18	6.0
2	6.0	19	12.0
3	6.0	20	6.0
4	12.0	21	12.0
5	6.0	22	6.0
6	6.0	23	1.5
7	2–6	24	6.0
8	6–12	30	2–32
10	6–12	31	24.0
11	6.0	32	12–32
16	110.0	33	24.0
17	110.0	33	120.0

supply for most situations. If the storage battery current is to be distributed to several laboratories, a maximum of twenty-four volts would be better. The higher voltage level would give the teacher a greater opportunity to do work which requires a steady current supply.

Other Sources of Low Voltage Direct Current.

The replies to Question 4 in Table 2 show that eighteen of the thirty teachers who reported are of the opinion that most of the low voltage DC work can be taken care of satisfactorily by dry cells or other primary cells, or by dry rectifiers like those for radio. Some of the reasons given by those who answered this question in the negative are: (1) dry cells deteriorate rapidly and are therefore expensive; (2) dry cells as well as wet primary cells have a small current capacity; (3) the dry rectifiers used for radio have too great variations in voltage under load changes. The replies to Question 7 of Table 2 indicate that many of the teachers were not familiar with the commercial wet primary cells. Eight of the seventeen who did reply to this question thought that the wet primary cells might be used in the place of dry cells and storage cells. The replies to this inquiry are not unusual because wet primary cells do not have the wide commercial use which they had in the past.

Motor-generator sets are available which furnish the low voltage DC as well as the high voltage. The larger power capacity outfits are generally built so that there is one AC motor to drive two DC generators, one generator for low voltage and the other for high voltage. For lower capacity motor-generator sets an AC motor drives a DC generator having double commutators to furnish the high and low voltages. Monahan [12] describes one of the latter type outfits which furnishes forty-five watts DC at six to eight volts and 200 watts at 110 volts. It must be remembered that low capacities at low voltages result when the motor-generator set is so designed that the low voltage DC is obtained when only the residual magnetism in the field coils of the generator is effective. As previously stated, most physics teachers want a motor-generator set for use in the first course. The following question was asked with reference to a probable advanced course in physics. "If a motor-generator set were

[12] Monahan, A. C., *op. cit.*, p. 23.

available could all of the remaining DC work be done well by
using portable storage cells?" The data in the fourth column
of Table 6 show that nineteen of the twenty-one who made
definite replies did so in the affirmative. The type of motor
generator and the kind of advanced course offered are important
factors to be considered. In any event the replies received indicate that a motor-generator set of proper design is a very important item of the power supply equipment.

Sources of Low Voltage Alternating Current.

When ordinary house lighting power supply furnishes alternating current it is an easy matter to get any voltage level
desired by the use of transformers. Since the amperage required
at voltage levels much below 110 volts is small the power capacity of the transformer may be small. For most work a fraction
of a kilowatt is sufficient. The transformer should be provided
with taps from which different voltage levels can be drawn. The
number of taps used would depend upon the size of the voltage
steps desired. This in turn would depend upon the resistance
equipment available for fine regulation. The smaller the voltage
step the less the amount of resistance necessary for fine regulation. One very convenient arrangement is to place the taps so
that four or five volt steps are obtained. For most of the work
in the first course in physics no fine regulation is necessary,
especially if ordinary laboratory resistance equipment is available. Sometimes the entire voltage variation is obtained by the
use of resistances. This practice is not economical, particularly
where much current is drawn, because of the large amount of
energy which is lost in the resistances. In case direct current is
supplied to the entire building for the power and lighting circuits it is necessary to use either commercial equipment in the
form of a motor generator or a rotary converter, or laboratory
equipment in the form of an AC generator. Many physics
teachers believe that there is little place for the study of alternating currents in the first course in physics. For those teachers
a demonstration model of AC generator would be satisfactory.
Many excellent demonstration models are on the market now.
It is difficult to understand why the study of alternating currents
should be omitted from the course in physics since this is the
kind of electricity most commonly used.

The High Voltage (110 and above) AC Supply.

In most communities to-day the electric power service station furnishes AC to the subscribers at either 110 or 220 volt levels. In either case it is simply a matter of proper wiring to get the 110 volt level. If only 110 volts are furnished the 220 volt level and, in fact, any other volt level can be obtained by the use of transformers.

Since three-phase induction motors are used so commonly for machine drives the central power stations have been forced to supply three-phase AC. This is generally at the 220 volt level. In some places where extremely heavy loads occur the 440 volt level is common. It is therefore generally easy to get the three-phase supply for the laboratory. In case no commercial supply is available it is still easy to obtain this kind of AC from such laboratory generators as have been placed on the market by several apparatus houses. The laboratory units would be used for experimental or demonstration purposes only and therefore would not require much capacity. Where the three-phase AC is supplied to the panel board, provision should be made for each phase to be drawn off independently, thus making the arrangement adaptable to study purposes.

The High Voltage (110 and above) DC Supply.

Unless the entire building is supplied with direct current it is customary to obtain it from a motor-generator set consisting of an AC motor and one or more DC generators. As previously stated in connection with the discussion of the low voltage DC supply, some motor-generator outfits furnish the DC at several voltage levels. Many physics departments have motor generators which by resistance regulation will furnish direct current at voltage levels ranging from approximately 90 to 150 volts. DC voltage levels higher than these can be obtained from motor generators or in the form of rectified AC. The difficulty which arises from the use of most types of rectifiers to furnish the DC to the physics department from an AC supply is that electrical power capacities of these devices are too small when decided variation in the load is produced. In spite of this, there is a definite place for this kind of equipment, especially where finances prohibit the installation of motor-generator sets and storage batteries.

Facilities Now Furnished on Master Panel Boards.

The second to seventh columns of Table 12 give data relative to services which are found in connection with the master panel board equipment in the 30 schools from which reports were received. This table indicates that only about one-third of the schools have storage batteries connected with the central panel board. In 22 of the 30 schools motor-generator sets are a part of the equipment. In only 7 schools are bulb chargers installed

TABLE 12

SERVICES FOR WHICH PROVISIONS ARE NOW MADE IN THE PANEL BOARD EQUIPMENT

Replies to Questionnaire

School Number	Storage Battery	Motor Generator	Bulb Charger	Plugs to Table Circuits	Switches to Table Circuits	Transformer
2		X		X	X	
3		X			X	
4	X	X	X	X	X	X
5		X			X	
6		X			X	
7	X	X		X	X	
8	X	X			X	
9		X			X	
10		X			X	
11				X		
12		X			X	
13		X	X	X	X	
14		X		X	X	
15		X			X	
17					X	
18	X		X		X	
19	X	X	X	X		
20		X			X	
21	X	X	X		X	
22				X	X	
23					X	
24		X		X		
25		X			X	
30	X	X		X	X	X
31	X	X	X	X	X	
33	X	X		X		
34	X	X	X		X	

on the panel board. There were only 2 cases of transformers being permanently mounted on the power distribution board.

The returns indicate that switches are more frequently used than plugs for connecting power supply to the table circuits. Table 12 shows that there are 23 cases of the former and 12 of the latter. In some places switches are used for part of the service, like 110 volts alternating current, and plugs for the low voltage direct current service. Unpopularity of plugs in the past has been due to several causes. In the first place the ordinary plugs wear so rapidly that they will not make good contact after they have been in service for a short time. The writer was informed that this is one of the important reasons that winged nuts instead of plugs were recommended for use on the new standard panel boards for the high schools in New York City. Plugs with a gradual taper will last much longer than those with a sharp taper. The new-type split plug and receptacle seem to make good contact and they appear to have good lasting qualities. The cost of manufacturing good plugs is another reason for not using them. When plugs are used it is easier to make wrong connections than when the circuits are permanently connected to switches. Where these difficulties can be overcome, plugs and cords furnish a very flexible and convenient means for connecting the circuits on the panel board. The new commercial panel boards which are built for school use and which meet the requirements of the National Board of Fire Underwriters' laboratories have special cords and plugs which are used to connect the 110 volt level energy to the table outlets on the board. Each pair of terminals is fastened in a holder so that there is little chance for short circuits. The arrangement is similar to that in an ordinary plug used for connecting household appliances to the screw receivers which fit into the sockets of the lighting circuit. In fact, one manufacturer uses a heavy duty plug of exactly this design.

Visits to new high school buildings revealed a tendency to install commercial panel boards. The items of equipment generally associated with them are: (1) small motor generator ($\frac{3}{4}$ to $1\frac{1}{2}$ kilowatt) to give DC voltages from about 90 to 125; (2) storage battery, twelve to twenty-four volts, and thirty to eighty ampere-hour capacities; (3) battery charging equipment, usually a bulb type; (4) taps from the storage battery so that various voltages can be obtained in steps of two or four volts; (5) 110 volt AC supply from house circuits; (6) plugs or switches to table circuits; (7) fuses and circuit breakers; and (8) meters.

Important considerations regarding panel board equipment and installation are given in Appendix C.

SUMMARY

1. The following are some tendencies in science teaching: (a) to include a large number of practical topics, and to have pupils think in terms of life situations; (b) to place an increasing amount of emphasis on teacher demonstrations; (c) to encourage a broad choice of subject matter, especially for enrichment cases; and (d) to employ a variety of teaching methods.

2. Only 18 of the 30 teachers believe that an advanced course in high school physics will be offered in the comprehensive high school unless special emphasis is to be placed on technical courses.

3. Physics will probably be an elective subject in most non-technical high schools.

4. It is customary in many schools to have two pupils work together on an average physics experiment, and to use the laboratory for about two-thirds or less of the school day.

5. In general, portable tables and wall outlets for electricity are not favored in a physics laboratory set-up.

6. Few physics teachers favor the use of portable motor-generator sets mounted on trucks.

7. The contents of laboratory manuals and the replies of physics teachers indicate that 13 or 14 represent a reasonable average for the number of student experiments which require electricity in the first course in high school.

8. A maximum of 20 amperes is ample for the AC requirements for the physics laboratories in 77 per cent of the schools from which reports were received. The most common amperage reported for the first course in physics is fifteen, and fifty for the advanced course.

9. Most of the power from the AC source is at the 110 volt level; 220 volts are seldom needed for work in the first course in physics. The majority of those teachers who reported were of the opinion that an advanced course would require the use of more electric power at the 220 volt level than is essential for the work in the first course.

10. According to all sources of information checked, single-phase AC is necessary in a physics laboratory. Some three-phase AC is desirable, but not necessary.

11. Replies to questionnaires indicate that for a first course in physics, the laboratory should be supplied with DC at 110-150 volt levels and also at twelve to fifteen volt levels. Laboratory manuals, courses of study, and lists of apparatus reveal a need for only such DC as can be obtained from a maximum of seven Number 6 dry cells or six to twelve volt storage battery supply. Higher voltages would be required for an advanced course.

12. For the usual first course in physics a DC supply to the laboratory of twenty to twenty-five amperes would be ample. For an advanced course fifty amperes would be desirable.

13. All sources of information indicate that the lecture-room should be supplied with AC at 110 volt and 220 volt levels along with some provision for obtaining lower voltages when desired.

14. An AC supply of twenty amperes capacity is ample for all the demonstrations except those rather unusual ones which involve the use of large arc furnaces or arc lights.

15. Single-phase AC is a necessary part of the lecture-room power supply; three-phase AC is desirable.

16. For lecture-room work DC should be supplied at voltages from 110 down.

17. A maximum of thirty amperes DC would be ample for demonstrations according to the content of textbooks and courses of study, as well as the replies of 14 of the 18 teachers questioned.

18. According to the teachers questioned the physics shop should be supplied with 110 volts AC and DC, and three-phase 220 volts AC. A maximum of twenty amperes is ample for any of the kinds of electric power furnished. If the department has a panel board, all kinds of power available at the panel board should be supplied to outlets in the shop.

19. Replies to questionnaires indicate the following: (1) two teachers favor nickel-iron (alkali storage cells to every one who favors the lead-sulphuric acid type; (2) sixteen prefer the use of a motor generator for charging storage batteries against six who prefer the bulb charger; (3) twenty-one from a total of twenty-nine believe that except for a few portables, storage cells could be omitted from the power supply equipment for the first course in physics.

20. Lead-sulphuric acid cells are cheaper than nickel-iron cells, but nickel-iron cells will stand greater abuse.

21. Questionnaire replies show: (1) that motor generators are more common than storage batteries as a part of the equipment associated with the central panel board; (2) transformers are seldom a part of the panel board equipment; (3) switches rather than plugs are used generally for interconnecting circuits.

22. Most of the master panels and distribution panels now being installed in high school physics departments are designed so that the current supplies and the table circuits can be connected as desired by the use of flexible cords fitted with plug or lug terminals.

23. There is a marked tendency to equip high school physics departments with panel boards from which the electric power is distributed by means of permanent wiring to desired stations throughout the department. In many cases the electric power supply for other science laboratories is obtained from the physics master panel. These panels have facilities for furnishing power from AC and DC generators and from batteries.

24. Two reasons given for not favoring the general use of dry cells are: they deteriorate rapidly and are therefore expensive; they have a small current capacity.

25. The general use of dry rectifiers is not favored because of their great variations in voltages under load changes.

26. Both the low and the high voltages DC can be obtained from motor generators.

27. Transformers having a number of taps on the secondary windings offer convenient means of obtaining low and high voltages AC.

28. Polyphase AC can be obtained from: (1) the city service; (2) use of transformers; (3) commercial or demonstration generators.

29. Because of the common use of electricity in life situations and the rapid developments taking place in the science of electricity, the electric power requirements necessary to perform the experiments suggested in textbooks, courses of study, and laboratory manuals should be considered no better than minimum requirements.

CHAPTER V

ELECTRIC POWER SUPPLY FOR CHEMISTRY, BIOLOGY, AND GENERAL SCIENCE ROOMS

The purpose of this chapter is to point out the electric power requirements for the work in chemistry, biology, and general science and to show how these requirements can be met. These three sciences are treated in the same chapter because the electric power requirements for the work in these three subjects is small compared with the requirements for the work in physics. Many of the details of the equipment used to furnish the necessary power are the same whether they are used for one subject or another. Suggested installations for electric power supply to the science rooms are given in Appendix C.

CHEMISTRY

Power Requirements for the Chemistry Laboratory.

Table 13 shows what electric power is now used in the chemistry laboratories in the twenty schools from which reports were received. This same table shows what the teacher who made the report believes should be furnished. The second column of this table indicates that alternating current is used in only a few schools and that where an alternating current supply is furnished it is at the 110 volt level. The data in the fourth column show that the 110 volt AC supplies are furnished at a maximum of 15 amperes. According to the data in the third column of this table few teachers are desirous of having AC available in the chemistry laboratory. Those who do want the AC are all in favor of the 110 volt level, one teacher would like to have the 10 to 20 volt levels in addition, while one believes that as high as 220 volts would be desirable. A maximum of 15 amperes would meet the desired alternating current requirements for all but one of these teachers. This teacher would like to have as high as 100 amperes AC available.

140

TABLE 13

CHEMISTRY LABORATORY POWER REQUIREMENTS

Replies to Questionnaire

School Number	Alternating Current				Direct Current			
	Volts		Amperes		Volts		Amperes	
	Using	Desired	Using	Desired	Using	Desired	Using	Desired
1	0	110	0	4–6	0	10	0	4–6
2					110		20	
3	6–110							
4	110	10	15	15	24	24	15	20
5					0–110	0–110	0–10	0–10
7	110	110	5–15	5–15	4–8	4–8	10	10
8					115	115	10	10
9					0–110		0–10	
10	0	10–20 / 110–220	0	100–50 / 25–15	110	6–15–110	25	100–50–25
11	Dry cells and city supply							
12					0–110	0–110	0–10	0–10
13					110	110	0–5	0–5
14					110		House	
15					110	110	20	20
16					110		50	
17					110	110	10	10
					5–10			50
29					110			

The data in the sixth, seventh, eighth, and ninth columns of Table 13 indicate that direct current (DC) is used more frequently than alternating current (AC). In the sixth and eighth columns are data which show that in most places the DC power supply is at 110 volts with a maximum of about ten amperes. In most of the places where the 110 volt level DC is used there is an electric power plant which supplies power for the entire building. In a few cases DC is obtained from the city power plant. These situations probably account for the use of the comparatively high voltage and amperage levels. The values given in the seventh and ninth columns of Table 13 show that 110 volts and at least ten amperes are desired by most of the teachers. This may be accounted for by the probability that these teachers do not wish to change the experiments which have been planned especially for this kind of power supply. Where the 110 volt level is supplied to the entire building, it is very convenient to use it for the chemistry laboratory experiments. This is true also when the power supply is obtained from a central distribution point already equipped to furnish the high voltage DC. The latter arrangement is quite common in the schools which the writer visited. In fact, in some of the new high schools in New York City the power supply equipment for the chemistry laboratory is almost as elaborate as that for the physics laboratory. It is interesting to note that five of the teachers who now have the 110 volt level DC available did not express a desire for it. The specifications [1] for chemistry room equipment in the New York City high schools require provisions for supplying to the laboratory direct current of the 110 volt level, storage battery current and AC if desired.

Many of the chemistry teachers who were interviewed did not use electrical power in connection with any of the experiments assigned to the pupils. In fact, no teachers were requiring experiments in the first course in chemistry which could not be conducted satisfactorily with a DC supply such as is obtainable from a six volt storage battery or a maximum of four Number 6 dry cells.

In order to get a further check on the actual power requirements for chemistry experiments the author studied three widely used chemistry laboratory manuals.[2] In the manual by Brownlee and others, only two of the eighty-four experiments given required the use of electric power. These were the experiments on the electrolysis of water and on direct decomposition. In the write-up for the electrolysis experiment two arrangements were suggested, one employed the use of three dry cells in series and the other provided for connecting through a 100 watt lamp resistance to a 110 volt DC supply. The experiment on direct decomposition was similar to the electrolysis experiment. In

[1] *Specifications for Standard Arrangement and Equipment of Chemistry Rooms in High Schools of the City of New York.* Approved by the Board of Superintendence, June 14, 1926. Mimeographed copy.

[2] Brownlee, R. B., Fuller, R. W., Hancock, W. J., Sohon, M. N. and Whitsit, J. E. *Laboratory Exercises.* (Rev. Ed.) Allyn and Bacon, 1928.

Bruce, G. H. *A Laboratory Manual of Chemistry.* World Book Company, Yonkers-on-Hudson, New York, 1924.

Gray, C. W. and Sandifer, C. W. *Laboratory Manual.* Houghton Mifflin Company, 1924.

the laboratory manual by Bruce no experiments were given which require the use of electricity. Of the eighty-four experiments given in the manual by Gray and Sandifer only four required the use of electricity. One of these was a demonstration experiment and for the two others regular house supply could be used. The experiment on alloys included the use of a soldering iron which might be operated from the regular house supply, either 110 volts AC or 110 volts DC. This experiment could be performed without the use of an electric soldering iron. The experiment on the physical properties of water required the use of 110 volts DC. For the electrolysis of water experiment a six to twelve volt DC supply was suggested. The other experiment was on photography and required the use of a dark room equipped with electric lamps supplied with power from the ordinary house-lighting circuits. Many instructors require their pupils to do experiments other than those given in the published laboratory manuals. In some schools experiments are given which require the determination of electrochemical equivalents and a study of the process of electroplating. Since these experiments are performed in the chemistry laboratory, only low voltages and small amperages are required. One six volt storage battery or several dry cells will generally suffice.

As a still further check on the electrical power requirements the writer examined the lists of apparatus drawn up by the Central Scientific Company [3] for the high school chemistry work required by each of the forty-eight states. The lists give nothing in the way of power supply equipment except dry cells. The maximum number of dry cells called for in any list is fifteen, in most cases only two or three dry cells are required. Many of the lists include the electrolysis apparatus which can be operated on a low voltage small current supply. These lists do not give motor-driven stirrers, ball mills, vacuum pressure pumps, etc. Most of the motor-driven machinery which might be used in the chemistry laboratory could be equipped with universal (AC or DC) motors which would operate on the house power supply. Monahan's [4] list includes no experiments having greater power requirements than those given above.

If electric furnaces are to be used in the laboratory, a reason-

[3] *Standard State Lists of High School Laboratory Equipment.* Central Scientific Company, Chicago, 1927.
[4] Monahan, A. C., *op. cit.*

ably high wattage should be available. Some popular types of arc furnaces which draw 15 to 45 amperes can be connected directly to the 110 volt supply. The different types of muffle furnaces used in schools require from 800 to 6,000 watts, depending upon the size of the furnace and the temperature desired. Crucible furnaces consume approximately 370 to 500 watts. If an AC power supply is available it is generally best to use a stepdown transformer of the proper capacity and to connect the primary of the transformer to a 220 or 440 volt supply. Electrolysis, electroplating, and electroanalysis experiments can be performed successfully with fifteen volts DC.

The above discussion indicates that practically all the experiments commonly required in the first course in chemistry can be performed without any more electric power than is obtainable from a few dry cells or a six volt storage battery and the AC supply from the lighting circuit.

In the chemical industries extensive use is made of electricity It seems reasonable to believe that the future developments of experimental work in chemistry will include studies of some of the many practical electrochemical processes.

Power Requirements for the Chemistry Lecture-Room

The power requirements for the lecture and demonstration work in chemistry are not radically different from those for the chemistry laboratory in places where the laboratory work is emphasized. This situation is reflected when one compares the data in Table 14 with those in Table 13. Only three of the teachers reported power requirements different for the lecture work from those for the laboratory work. In only one school did the teacher have AC available in the lecture-room and not in the laboratory. This teacher believes that 110 volt AC with a maximum of thirty amperes is desirable in both places. Nearly all the teachers use low voltage DC. This is indicated by the fact that low voltage values are stated or ranges are given which include the low voltages near 10 to 15 volts. In four schools where the 110 volt level DC is available the teachers have not expressed a desire for it. This seems to indicate that if either high or low voltage DC must be omitted it would be advisable to omit the high voltage. One teacher desires a high amperage while three other teachers who now have high amperage

TABLE 14

CHEMISTRY LECTURE-ROOM POWER REQUIREMENTS

Replies to Questionnaire

SCHOOL NUMBER	ALTERNATING CURRENT				DIRECT CURRENT			
	Volts		Amperes		Volts		Amperes	
	Using	Desired	Using	Desired	Using	Desired	Using	Desired
1	0	110	0	4–6	0	10	0	4–6
2					110		20	
3	6–110							
4	110	110	15	15	24	24	15	20
5					0–110	0–110	0–10	0–10
6	110	110	30	30	6–110	6–110	30	30
7	110	110	5–15	5–15	4–8	4–8	10	10
8					115	115	10	10
9					0–110		0–80	
10	0	10–20 / 110–220	0	100–50 / 25–15	110	6–15 / 110	25	100–50 / 25
11	Dry cells and city supply							
12					0–110	0–110	0–10	0–10
13					110	110	0–5	0–30
15					110	110	20	20
16					110		50	
17					110	110	10	10
27					0–110	0–110	1–4	1–4
29					5–10 / 110			

available express no desire for it. These data indicate that a maximum of 10 to 15 amperes will meet the requirements for the chemistry lecture and demonstration work in practically all the schools from which reports were received.

The electric power requirements as revealed by the content of textbooks was obtained by an examination of seven outstanding chemistry textbooks.[5] The topics treated in these books include

[5] Black, N. H. and Conant, J. B. *Practical Chemistry.* The Macmillan Company, New York, 1927.

Brownlee, R. B., Fuller, R. W., Hancock, W. J., Sohon, M. N. and Whitsit, J. E. *Elementary Principles of Chemistry.* Allyn and Bacon, 1921.

Bruce, G. H. *High School Chemistry.* World Book Company, 1928.

Dull, C. E. *High School Chemistry.* Henry Holt and Company, 1925.

Emery, F. B., Downey, E. F., Davis, R. E., Boynton, C. E. *Chemistry in Everyday Life.* Lyons and Carnahan, New York, 1928.

Gray, C. W., Sandifer, C. W., Hanna, H. J. *Fundamentals of Chemistry.* Houghton Mifflin Company, 1924.

Holmes, H. N., Mattern, L. W. *Elements of Chemistry.* The Macmillan Company, 1927.

many applications of electricity in industrial chemistry. Very high voltages such as those produced by induction coils could be used in the study of X-rays, Alpha rays, cathode rays, preparation of ozone, and Cottrell dust precipitation. All the books contained considerable material dealing with ionization with special reference to electrolysis of such substances as water, hydrochloric acid, copper sulphate, and aluminum oxide. A method for determining the relative conductivities of solutions is given in all these books. Electric cells of various types are discussed. Many processes are described which involve the use of electric furnaces. Each of the books has a description of the Hall aluminum furnace. Some of the books contain discussions of the use of the electric arc for preparation of colloids and for the fixation of nitrogen. Photography is discussed to some extent in all the books. Bomb calorimeters, spectroscopes, optical pyrometers, eudiometers, and rectifiers are described in some of the textbooks. This study indicates that the subject matter included in modern chemistry textbooks presents many opportunities for the use of electricity in connection with the lecture-demonstration work. The different processes described include demands for large ranges in amperages and voltages, especially for DC. Little need for alternating current is indicated.

Although the content of textbooks indicates the possibility of using electricity extensively in the demonstration work, interviews indicate that most teachers of high school chemistry prefer to use pictures and diagrams to explain those processes which require the use of much electric power. It is difficult for the writer to understand why many of the common electrochemical processes are not demonstrated to the chemistry pupils. The use of electricity in the chemical industries is very extensive. It therefore seems reasonable to expect teachers to give an increasing amount of time to the study of electrochemical processes. The facilities for the electric power supply should be sufficiently flexible to provide for an increasing demand for demonstrations of electrochemical processes.

As a further check on the power requirements for the chemistry lecture-room, three courses of study [6] were examined for topics

[6] Committee Reports, *Chemistry for the High School*, Curriculum Bulletin, No. 32, Board of Education, City of St. Louis, 1926. Curriculum Revision Committee, *Senior High School Chemistry*, Denver Public Schools, 1927. *Tentative Course of Study in Chemistry for Secondary Schools in Indiana.* Bulletin N100 E-6, State Department of Public Instruction.

which involve the use of electricity. The following topics were suggested: electrolysis of water, electrolysis of aluminum oxide, preparation of flourine by electrolysis, electrolytic refining of copper, electroplating, manufacture of steel by the electric process, electrical conductivity of solutions, and electric refrigerators. In the Indiana course of study there is a suggestion that the chemistry department be supplied with a rectifier of AC variable type and a six volt ninety ampere-hour storage battery. This electric power supply when combined with the house supply of AC would be ample for work suggested in any of the courses of study.

In the standard specifications [7] for the New York City chemistry recitation rooms provisions are made for supplies of direct and alternating current of 50 amperes capacity (at 110 volt level) and storage battery current from twenty cells of 75 ampere-hour capacity.

Power Requirements for the Chemistry Preparation Room.

Table 15 shows that AC is available in the preparation rooms of only four of the twenty schools from which reports on chemistry power requirements were received. Only two teachers who do not have AC available expressed any desire for it in their work. Two teachers desire to have available AC voltages as high as 220. For all situations except one a maximum of fifteen amperes AC would be sufficient. Two teachers believe that as much as fifty amperes DC should be available. In fact, one of them desires 100 amperes. These high amperage requirements for preparation room work are unusual when only high school chemistry is taught. A maximum of ten amperes DC is usually sufficient.

If the electric power is obtained from a school power plant there is no serious difficulty involved in supplying high amperage, especially if the preparation rooms are near the generators. If DC must be obtained from small motor generators or from storage batteries a high wattage requirement would prove quite expensive. It would be better in situations like these to rely upon the city supply of AC and then use transformers in connection with the high wattage furnace work and induction motors

[7] *Specifications for Standard Arrangement and Equipment of Chemistry Rooms in High Schools, New York City.* Approved by the Board of Superintendents, June 14, 1926. Mimeographed copy, pp. 11-12.

TABLE 15

CHEMISTRY SHOP (PREPARATION ROOM) POWER REQUIREMENTS

Replies to Questionnaire

SCHOOL NUMBER	ALTERNATING CURRENT				DIRECT CURRENT			
	Volts		Amperes		Volts		Amperes	
	Using	Desired	Using	Desired	Using	Desired	Using	Desired
1	0	110	0	4–6	0		0	
2					110		20	
3	6–110							
4	110	110	15	15	24	24	15	20
5					0–110	0–110	0–10	0–10
7	110	110	5–15	5–15	4–8	4–8	10	10
8					115	15	10	10
9					0–110			0–50
10	0	10–20	0	100–50	110	6–15	25	100–50
		110–220		25–15		110		25
11	Dry cells and city supply							
12					0–110	0–110	0–10	0–10
15					110	110	20	20
16					110		50	
27					0–110	0–110	1–4	1–4
29					5–10			
					110			

for the machine drives. Portable storage batteries would be economical and convenient for low voltage high amperage DC.

When a master panel board is provided for the chemistry department it is sometimes placed in the preparation room. This is in accordance with the requirements of the New York City Standards [8] for high school chemistry department equipment. Any power which is supplied to the master panel board is available for use in the preparation room.

BIOLOGY

Power Requirements for the Biology Laboratory.

The data given in Table 16 indicate that the electric power supply for the biology laboratory work is comparatively small. Only five teachers of the sixteen from whom replies were ob-

[8] *Specifications for Standard Arrangement and Equipment of Chemistry Rooms in High Schools*, New York City. Mimeographed copy.

TABLE 16

BIOLOGY LABORATORY POWER REQUIREMENTS

Replies to Questionnaire

School Number	Alternating Current				Direct Current			
	Volts		Amperes		Volts		Amperes	
	Using	Desired	Using	Desired	Using	Desired	Using	Desired
1	0	110	0	5	0		0	
2					110		110	
4	110	110						
5					0–110	0–110	0–10	0–10
7	110		5–10					
8					115	115	10	10
10					110	110	25	25
12					0–110	0–110	0–10	?
13					110	110		
14					110		House	
16					110		50	
17					110	110	10	10
28	110	110	Commercial Supply		0	25	0	25 (?)

tained have or care to have AC available. Ten of the sixteen have DC available and most of these are in schools where each building has an electric power plant. The voltages and amperages given for both AC and DC are those most commonly available for ordinary house-lighting service, about 110 volts ten amperes.

Power supply such as can be obtained from the house-lighting circuits seems to be adequate for the work carried on in the biology laboratory, especially if supplemented with the power obtainable from a few dry cells or a storage battery. In some of the schools visited, the biology laboratory electric outlets were connected with the master panel board so that any power available for other science laboratories could be obtained in the biology laboratory. This arrangement becomes expensive when several laboratories are involved and when they are some distance away from the panel board.

In order to get a check on the ways in which electric power is used in the biology laboratory the writer employed four methods:

interviews with biology teachers in their laboratories; a study of widely used laboratory manuals for biology; review of state lists of apparatus; and study of the standard specifications for the New York City schools. The interviews and visitations revealed that about the only use that is ever made of electric power is to furnish energy for the light source of projection machines and for microscopic illuminators. Practically all projection and illumination equipment suitable for biology laboratory use is now designed for connecting directly with the 110 volt service. In some places where the electrolysis of water experiment is given it is customary to have about four dry cells or a storage battery, unless the house supply is DC, so that a resistance can be used to reduce the voltage to a suitable value.

In the laboratory guide by Clement [9] there are no experiments which require the use of electricity, except in connection with projection or microscope illumination. Of the 145 exercises given in the manual by Gruenberg and Wheat [10] only the experiment on the electrolysis of water specifically requires the use of electric power. The instructions for this experiment suggest the use of either 110 volts DC with an acid-water resistance, or four dry cells, or a storage battery.

The state lists of laboratory equipment [11] and Monahan's [12] list give only dry cells and storage batteries. Four dry cells for every twenty pupils is the maximum number recommended. One storage battery, usually 6 volts, is all that is ever mentioned. Few state lists give the storage battery.

The New York City specifications [13] for equipment of biology rooms call for only two electric outlets, one on the demonstration desk and one at the rear of the room. Both of these outlets are to be in the laboratory. No mention is made of provisions for supplying different types of current to the biology demonstration table outlet.

These findings indicate that outlets supplied with 110 volts DC or AC should be provided so that they are conveniently located

[9] Clement, A. G. *A Laboratory Guide and Note Book in Biology.* Iroquois Publishing Co., Inc., Syracuse, N. Y., 1925.

[10] Gruenberg, B. C., and Wheat, F. M. *Students' Manual of Exercises in Elementary Biology.* Ginn and Company, 1921.

[11] Standard State Lists of High School Laboratory Equipment.

[12] Monahan, A. C., *op. cit.*

[13] *Specifications for Standard Arrangement and Equipment of Biology Rooms in High Schools, New York City.* Approved by Board of Superintendents, June 21, 1926. Mimeographed copy.

for the use of projection apparatus and microscope illuminators. The remainder of the power needs should be cared for by a few dry cells or a six volt storage battery. There is no real need for connecting the biology laboratory outlets with a master panel board.

Power Requirements for the Biology Lecture-Room.

In many schools the biology lecture and demonstration work is carried on in the laboratory. Therefore one would expect that the power requirements reported for the lecture-room would be like those for the laboratory. The data given in Table 17 compared with those in Table 16 indicate that for those teachers who made reports the laboratory and lecture-room power requirements are the same.

TABLE 17

BIOLOGY LECTURE-ROOM POWER REQUIREMENTS

Replies to Questionnaire

SCHOOL NUMBER	ALTERNATING CURRENT				DIRECT CURRENT			
	Volts		Amperes		Volts		Amperes	
	Using	Desired	Using	Desired	Using	Desired	Using	Desired
1	0	110	0	5	0		0	
2					110		10	
4	110	110						
5					0–110	0–110	0–10	0–10
7	110		5–10					
8					115	115	10	10
12					0–110	0–110	0–10	
13					110	110		
28	110	110	Commercial Supply		0	25	0	25 (?)

It is possible that special provisions should be made in connection with demonstration work for the use of micro-projectors. Most good micro-projectors require comparatively high amperage supplied to their light sources. These amperages range from approximately four to thirty, depending upon the make of instrument used. Recent improvements in lens systems have made it possible to produce good micro-projectors which can be connected directly to the lighting circuit. These projectors require an amperage of four to ten. If much micro-projection and opaque projection is done, approximately 1,000 watts should be provided for each outfit.

A careful study of six textbooks [14] revealed no real need for electricity beyond that required for projection machines and microscope illuminators. X-ray pictures were included in some of the textbooks, but there was no indication that X-ray apparatus should be used in connection with demonstration. The New York City specifications [15] call for no special electric outlets in the biology recitation rooms.

Power Requirements for the Biology Preparation Room.

As indicated in Table 18 all the power requirements for the biology preparation room can be met by the use of the ordinary

TABLE 18

BIOLOGY SHOP (PREPARATION ROOM) POWER REQUIREMENTS

Replies to Questionnaire

SCHOOL NUMBER	ALTERNATING CURRENT				DIRECT CURRENT			
	Volts		Amperes		Volts		Amperes	
	Using	Desired	Using	Desired	Using	Desired	Using	Desired
1	0	110	10	5	0		0	
2					110		10	
4	110	110						
5					0–110	0–110	0–10	0–10
7	110		5–10					
8					115	115	10	10
12					0–110	0–110	0–10	
16					110		50	

[14] Atwood, W. H. *Biology.* P. Blakiston's Sons and Co., 1927.

Hunter, G. W. *New Civic Biology.* American Book Company, 1926.

Kinsey, A. C. *An Introduction to Biology.* J. B. Lippincott Company, Philadelphia, 1926.

Peabody, J. E., and Hunt, A. E. *Biology and Human Welfare.* The Macmillan Company, 1925.

Smallwood, W. M., Reveley, I. L., Bailey, G. A. *New Biology.* Allyn and Bacon, 1924.

Waggoner, H. D. *Modern Biology: Its Human Aspects.* D. C. Heath & Co., 1926.

[15] *Specifications for Standard Arrangement and Equipment of Biology Rooms in High Schools, City of New York.*

house-lighting supply. It is important to provide sufficient wall outlets with which to connect such equipment as sterilizers and slide illuminators. The New York City specifications for the biology preparation room call for one outlet above the wall table for sterilizers, etc., one at the work bench and one at the teacher's desk for desk light. The ordinary sterilizer requires less than 200 watts and can be connected directly to the lighting service. Fractional horse-power motors which operate from the 110 volt supply are generally powerful enough for any motor-driven machine used in the biology preparation room.

GENERAL SCIENCE

Power Requirements for the General Science Laboratory.

Analyses of textbooks in general science made by Downing [16] and his students and by Webb [17] show that textbooks in general science, particularly the more recent ones, are made up of content selected from all the fields of science. The objectives of the author are to give such instruction as will enable students to interpret the science of their environment. This points to the need for electrical equipment for the general science classroom which will permit such flexibility as will enable the teacher to portray common applications of electricity.

The data in Table 19 indicate that the schools covered include both types of courses. Two teachers reported that no electric power was available for experimental use in the general science laboratories. One teacher said that an adequate supply of electric power could be obtained from dry cells. With the exception of those schools where the power supply from the physics laboratory is available there are only three schools in which alternating current is supplied to the general science laboratories for experimental use. The voltage level of this supply is approximately 110. This same voltage level is common for the DC supply also. In many cities the electric power for general use in each large high school is supplied by DC generators operated as part of the school plant. In most schools where 110 volts DC is supplied to a laboratory, facilities are at hand for reducing

[16] Overn, O. E.; Iler, Ernest; Heinemann, Ailsie; and Downing, E. R. "An Analysis of Textbooks in General Science." *General Science Quarterly*, May 1928, Vol. XII, No. 4, pp. 509-16.

[17] Webb, H. A. *Graphic Chart of the Eighteen General Science Textbooks Published or Revised Since 1917.* Distributed by the author.

TABLE 19

GENERAL SCIENCE LABORATORY POWER REQUIREMENTS

Replies to Questionnaire

SCHOOL NUMBER	ALTERNATING CURRENT				DIRECT CURRENT			
	Volts		Amperes		Volts		Amperes	
	Using	Desired	Using	Desired	Using	Desired	Using	Desired
2					110		30	
3	6–110							
5					0–110	0–110	0–10	0–10
7	110		5–10					
8		115–120		10	0–12 0–115	115	10	10
10	0	110	0		110	6–15–110	25	25
11	Dry cells all that are needed							
12					0–110	0–110	0–10	
13					110	110		
14					110		House Supply	
15					110	110	20	10
25	Use physics rooms							
28	110	110	Commercial		0	25	0	25

this voltage to lower levels so that almost any voltage between 0 and 110 can be obtained.

In some of the schools visited, the facilities for supplying power to the general science laboratories were practically as elaborate as those in the physics laboratories.

In order not to be biased by judgments formed as a result of observations and interviews the writer noted every topic treated in three recent general science books [18] to determine what electric power was really needed to perform any experiments which might be suggested. All such topics as resistance and heat, bells, wire resistance, ways of connecting cells, storage cells, motors, electromagnetism, electroplating, electrolysis, and wiring can be handled successfully with the regular power supply from a

[18] Pieper, C. J. and Beauchamp, W. L. *Everyday Problems in Science*. Scott, Foresman, and Company, 1927.

Wood, G. C. and Carpenter, H. A. *Our Environment: How We Use and Control It*. Allyn and Bacon, 1928.

Caldwell, O. W. and Eikenberry, W. L., *Elements of General Science, With Experiments*. Ginn and Company, 1926.

house-lighting circuit and a source of low voltage DC like three dry cells or one six volt storage battery.

A check of the lists of equipment for general science given in the Central Scientific Company [19] publication and the bulletin prepared by Monahan [20] did not reveal any need for electric power supply in excess of that obtainable from the facilities given in the preceding paragraph.

The specifications [21] for standard arrangement and equipment of the general science department of New York City high schools make such provisions that the general science rooms may be used as combination laboratories and recitation rooms. All types of current are to be supplied to the demonstration tables. Special emphasis is placed on a twenty-five volt DC supply for the laboratory tables and the pupils' tables. The laboratory table has one outlet for stereopticon.

Power Requirements for the General Science Lecture-Room.

A comparison of the data in Tables 19 and 20 shows that a somewhat more elaborate power supply is furnished for lecture and demonstration work than for laboratory. This is as one would expect because so much of the experimental work in general science is done as demonstrations by the teacher. If the requirements of the teachers who replied to the questionnaire are to be met, it will be necessary to supply both AC and DC at the 110 volt level. For both kinds of currents several voltage levels below 110 are suggested. A maximum of twenty to twenty-five amperes will be sufficient to meet most of the requirements.

The power supply called for in the preceding paragraph is in excess of that required to carry out the work suggested in any of the textbooks referred to on page 154, or to use the equipment given in the Central Scientific Company's list and Monahan's list. As previously stated, the instructor has such a broad field from which to choose topics that unusual power requirements might be justified.

The results indicate that provision should be made for 110 volt AC probably directly from the house-lighting circuit, and

[19] Central Scientific Company, *op. cit.*

[20] Monahan, A. C., *Laboratory Layouts for the High School Sciences.* Bulletin 1927, No. 22. U. S. Bureau of Education.

[21] *Specifications for Standard Arrangement and Equipment of General Science Departments in High School.* Approved by Board of Superintendents, New York City, April 22, 1926. Mimeographed copy.

for low voltage DC, the upper limit being determined largely by the power available from other sources such as physics laboratory generators or the school power plant.

Power Requirements for the General Science Shop.

The data in Table 21 indicate that those teachers who replied to the questionnaire do not use much electric power in the general science shop. Moreover, these teachers do not believe that much electric power is necessary. The 110 volt level for both AC and DC seems to be in the greatest demand. Although 110 volts DC is mentioned more frequently than 110 volts AC, it must be remembered that a number of these schools have their own power plants which generate DC. Probably the correct statement of the situation is that the general science shop should be supplied with power from the regular house-lighting circuits. A sufficient number of outlets should be provided that the instructor can use such equipment as small motors, soldering irons, and small electric heaters.

TABLE 20

GENERAL SCIENCE LECTURE-ROOM POWER REQUIREMENTS

Replies to Questionnaire

SCHOOL NUMBER	ALTERNATING CURRENT				DIRECT CURRENT			
	Volts		Amperes		Volts		Amperes	
	Using	Desired	Using	Desired	Using	Desired	Using	Desired
2					110		30	
3	6–110							
4	24–110 2–6	2–12			24	2–24		
5					0–110	0–110	0–10	0–10
6	110	110	30	30	6–110	6–110	Low	30
7	110		5–10					
8			115–120	10	115	115	10	10
9					0–110		0–80	
10	0	110	0		110	6–15–110	25	25
12					0–110	0–110	0–10	
13					110	110		
15					110	110	20	10
17					110	110	20	20
28	110	110	Commercial		0	25	0	25

TABLE 21

GENERAL SCIENCE SHOP (PREPARATION ROOM) POWER REQUIREMENTS

Replies to Questionnaire

SCHOOL NUMBER	ALTERNATING CURRENT				DIRECT CURRENT			
	Volts		Amperes		Volts		Amperes	
	Using	Desired	Using	Desired	Using	Desired	Using	Desired
2					110		30	
3	6–110							
5					0–110	0–110	0–10	0–10
7	110		5–10					
8			115–120	10	115	115	10	10
12					0–110	0–110	0–10	
15					110	110	20	10

The specifications [22] for the equipment of the general science rooms in the New York City high schools provide that the preparation room shall have one outlet from which all types of current are obtainable and other outlets for the regular house service to furnish power for lathes, mimeograph machines, and desk lamps.

SUMMARY OF CHEMISTRY

1. Replies to questionnaires indicate that the laboratory demands for AC can be met in most cases by a 110 volt 15 ampere supply. Some of the teachers desire ten to twenty volt levels as well as the 220 volt level. The maximum AC amperage mentioned is 100. The DC supply is apparently more important than the AC supply for the chemistry laboratory. Most of the teachers desire a DC supply capable of delivering ten amperes at 110 volts; probably because in many schools the lighting service is DC.

2. Visits and the study of laboratory manuals and lists of equipment show that: (1) few pupil experiments in chemistry require electricity; (2) the experiments can be performed satisfactorily with electric power supplied by the house-lighting

[22] *Specifications for Standard Arrangement and Equipment of General Science Departments in High School.* See footnote 21.

service supplemented by a few Number 6 dry cells or a six volt, thirty ampere-hour storage battery.

3. Replies to these questionnaires indicate that 110 volts 30 amperes AC should be available in the chemistry lecture-room, and that low voltage DC is more useful in lecture-room work than high voltage DC, especially if the house-lighting supply is AC.

4. The study of textbooks, courses of study, and equipment catalogues revealed the fact that much industrial chemistry involving the use of electricity is being introduced into the modern courses in high school chemistry. This tendency makes a large electric power demand reasonable, especially when electric furnaces are used. At the 110 volt level a supply of 50 amperes AC and DC would be ample for almost any situation. For the low voltage work a seventy-five ampere-hour storage battery of twelve or twenty-four volts would be adequate.

5. According to the replies from questionnaires, there is no real demand for sources of both AC and DC in the chemistry preparation room. In most instances the house-lighting power supply is ample.

SUMMARY OF BIOLOGY

1. For the experimental work in the biology laboratory there is need for very little electric power beyond that obtainable from the house-lighting supply. Three or four Number 6 dry cells are adequate for the low voltage DC demands.

2. Projection apparatus is useful for both laboratory and lecture-room work. Nearly all the projectors commonly used may be connected to a 110 volt supply either AC or DC from which they draw a maximum of about ten amperes. Some micro-projectors require 4 to 30 amperes from a DC supply. However, there are now on the market good micro-projectors which draw 4 to 10 amperes.

3. If sufficient electric power is supplied for the operation of projection equipment the additional power necessary can be obtained from dry cells or a small six volt storage battery.

4. The electric power obtainable from the house-lighting circuit is ample for the biology preparation room. If transformers and resistances are employed this electric power supply is adequate for operating sterilizers, small motors, and lighting equipment.

SUMMARY OF GENERAL SCIENCE

1. There is a tendency to use the same room for laboratory and recitation work in general science. In some schools the general science laboratory experiments are conducted in the physics laboratory.

2. The content of general science textbooks and the topics suggested in courses of study indicate a tendency to acquaint the child with the applications of electricity in the home and in industry. The extensive use of electricity in life situations seems to warrant giving considerable attention to electricity in the general science course.

3. There is a wide range in the facilities for electric power supply in different schools. Replies to questionnaires indicate that in some schools there is no particular power supply for the general science laboratory while in other schools the facilities are as elaborate as those in the physics laboratory.

4. The experiments suggested in general science textbooks can be performed by using such power as can be obtained from the house-lighting supply along with several Number 6 dry cells or a six volt storage battery of twenty ampere-hour capacity. These supplies of power would be ample for any of the apparatus given in the lists of equipment for general science laboratories. The standard specifications for the new high schools in New York City request a twenty-five volt DC supply for the demonstration tables and the pupils' tables.

5. Because of the broad field which the topics in the general science textbooks cover it is advisable to have facilities for furnishing to the demonstration tables all types of current which are available at the master panel board in the physics laboratory.

6. The general science shop or preparation room should have outlets supplied with power suitable for motor-driven lathes, mimeograph machines, etc. The house-lighting power supply will be sufficient in most schools. Where one or more master panel boards are a part of the science department equipment, the general science shop should be provided with an outlet which is connected with a master panel board.

BIBLIOGRAPHY

PART I

CRANDALL, I. B. AND MACKENZIE, D. "Analysis of the Energy Distribution in Speech." *Physical Review*, Vol. XIX, March 1922.

DUFF, J. C. "Radio as a Means to Instruction." *School Executives Magazine*, Vol. 43, No. 5, January 1929.

GOLDSMITH, A. N. AND MINTON, J. P. "The Performance and Theory of Loud Speaker Horns." *Proceedings, Institute of Radio Engineers*, Vol. 12, No. 4, August 1924.

HULL, L. M. "Over-all Measurements on Broadcast Receivers." *Proceedings of the Radio Club of America*, Vol. 5, No. 8, October 1928.

MORECROFT, JOHN H., PINTO, A. AND CURRY, W. A. *Principles of Radio Communication*. Second edition. John Wiley and Sons, Inc., New York, 1927.

RICE, C. W. AND KELLOGG, E. W. "Notes on the Development of a New Type Loud Speaker." *Journal of the American Institute of Electrical Engineers*, Vol. 44, September 1925.

SILVER, McMURDO. "Some Practical Data on Public Address Amplification." *Radio Engineering*, Vol. 8, No. 12, December 1928.

STEINBERG, JOHN C. "Fundamentals of Speech, Hearing and Music." *Bell Laboratories Record*, November 1928.

STOLLER, HUGH M. "Speed Control for the Sound Picture System." *Bell Laboratories Record*, November 1928.

VAN DYCK, A. F. AND ENGEL, F. H. "Vacuum Tube Production Tests." *Proceedings, Institute of Radio Engineers*, Vol. 16, November 1928. No. 11.

WENTE, E. C. "The Effect of the Acoustics of an Auditorium on the Interpretation of Speech." *The American Architect*, Vol. CXXXIV, No. 2551, August 20, 1928.

WOLFF, IRVING. "Some Measurements and Loud Speaker Characteristics." *Proceedings, Institute of Radio Engineers*, Vol. 16, No. 12, December 1928.

WOLFF, IRVING AND RINGEL, A. "Loud Speaker Testing Methods." *Proceedings, Institute of Radio Engineers*, Vol. 15, May 1927.

Definition of Terms and Graphic Symbols. Committee on Standards, Institute of Radio Engineers, 1926.

"Educational Broadcasting." *Report of a Special Investigation in the County of Kent During the Year 1927*. The Carnegie United Kingdom Trustees, Comely Park House, Dunfermline, 1928.

"National Electric Code." *Regulations of the National Board of Fire Underwriters for Electric Wiring and Apparatus.* 1928 Edition.

NATIONAL ELECTRICAL MANUFACTURERS' ASSOCIATION. *Handbook of Radio Standards.* Fourth edition. New York, 1928.

"Radio Lessons Put Penalty on Guessing." *School Topics,* Cleveland, Ohio, Vol. XI (April 9, 1929), No. 14.

WESTERN ELECTRIC COMPANY. *General Information for the Care and Operation of a Public Address System.* Instruction Bulletin, No. 177.

PART II

ATWOOD, W. H. *Biology.* P. Blakiston's Sons and Co., Philadelphia, 1927.

BLACK, N. H. *Laboratory Experiments in Practical Physics.* The Macmillan Company, New York, 1927.

BLACK, N. H. AND CONANT, J. B. *Practical Chemistry.* The Macmillan Company, 1927.

BLACK, N. H. AND DAVIS, H. N. *New Practical Physics.* The Macmillan Company, New York, 1929.

BROWNLEE, R. B., FULLER, R. W., HANCOCK, W. J., SOHON, M. N. AND WHITSIT, J. E. *Elementary Principles of Chemistry.* Allyn and Bacon, New York, 1921.

BROWNLEE, R. B., FULLER, R. W., HANCOCK, W. J., SOHON, M. N. AND WHITSIT, J. E. *Laboratory Exercises.* Revised edition. Allyn and Bacon, New York, 1928.

BRUCE, G. H. *High School Chemistry.* World Book Company, Yonkers-on-Hudson, N. Y., 1928.

BRUCE, G. H. *A Laboratory Manual of Chemistry.* World Book Company, Yonkers-on-Hudson, N. Y., 1924.

CALDWELL, O. W. AND EIKENBERRY, W. L. *Elements of General Science, with Experiments.* Ginn and Company, Boston, 1926.

CLEMENT, A. G. *A Laboratory Guide and Note Book in Biology.* Iroquois Publishing Company, Syracuse, N. Y., 1925.

DULL, C. E. *Modern Physics.* Henry Holt and Company, New York, 1928.

DULL, C. E. *High School Chemistry.* Henry Holt and Company, New York, 1925.

DULL, C. E. *Laboratory Exercises in Physics.* Henry Holt and Company, New York, 1929.

EMERY, F. B., DOWNEY, E. F., DAVIS, R. E. AND BOYNTON, C. E. *Chemistry in Everyday Life.* Lyons and Carnahan, New York, 1928.

FULLER, R. W., BROWNLEE, R. B. AND BAKER, D. L. *Laboratory Exercises in Physics.* Allyn and Bacon, New York, 1927.

FULLER, R. W., BROWNLEE, R. B. AND BAKER, D. L. *Elementary Principles of Physics.* Allyn and Bacon, New York, 1927.

GOOD, F. F. *Laboratory Projects in Physics.* The Macmillan Company, New York, 1923.

GRAY, C. W. AND SANDIFER, C. W. *Laboratory Manual.* Houghton Mifflin Company, Chicago, 1924.

GRAY, C. W., SANDIFER, C. W. AND HANNA, H. J. *Fundamentals of Chemistry.* Houghton Mifflin Company, Chicago, 1924.

GRUENBERG, B. C. AND WHEAT, F. M. *Students Manual of Exercises in Elementary Biology.* Ginn and Company, Boston, 1921.

HOLMES, H. N. AND MATTERN, L. W. *Elements of Chemistry.* The Macmillan Company, New York, 1927.

HORTON, R. E. *Measurable Outcomes from Laboratory Instruction.* Bureau of Publications, Teachers College, Columbia University, New York, 1928.

HUNTER, GEORGE W. "The Place of Science in the Secondary School." *School Review,* Vol. XXXIII (May-June 1925).

HUNTER, GEORGE W. *New Civic Biology.* American Book Company, New York, 1926.

KINSEY, A. C. *An Introduction to Biology.* J. B. Lippincott Company, Philadelphia, 1926.

MILLIKAN, R. A., GALE, H. G. AND DAVIS, I. C. *Exercises in Laboratory Physics for Secondary Schools.* Ginn and Company, Boston, 1925.

MILLIKAN, R. A., GALE, H. G. AND PYLE, W. R. *Elements of Physics.* Ginn and Company, Boston, 1927.

MONAHAN, A. C. *Laboratory Layouts for the High School Sciences.* Bulletin 1927, No. 22, U. S. Bureau of Education.

MORPHET, E. L. *The Measurement and Interpretation of School Building Utilization.* Bureau of Publications, Teachers College, Columbia University, New York, 1927.

OVERN, O. E., ILER, ERNEST, HEINEMAN, AILSIE AND DOWNING, E. R. "An Analysis of Textbooks in General Science." *General Science Quarterly,* Vol. XII, No. 4, May 1928.

PEABODY, J. E. AND HUNT, A. E. *Biology and Human Welfare.* The Macmillan Company, New York, 1925.

PIEPER, C. J. AND BEAUCHAMP, A. L. *Everyday Problems in Science.* Scott Foresman and Company, Chicago, 1927.

POWERS, S. R. "The Selection and Purchase of Equipment and Furnishings for Laboratories." *The American School and University Yearbook,* Second Annual Edition. American School Publishing Company, New York, 1929.

SEARS, F. E. *Laboratory Manual of Physics.* F. M. Ambrose and Company, Boston, 1928.

SMALLWOOD, W. M., REVELEY, I. L., BAILEY, G. A. *New Biology.* Allyn and Bacon, New York, 1924.

WAGGONER, H. D. *Modern Biology: Its Human Aspects.* D. C. Heath and Company, Boston, 1926.

WEBB, H. A. *Graphic Chart of the Eighteen General Science Textbooks Published or Revised since 1917.* Distributed by the author.

WISEHART, R. P. *Tentative Course of Study in Physics for the Secondary Schools of Indiana.* Bulletin 100 E-5. State Department of Public Instruction, 1928.

Wood, G. C. and Carpenter, H. A. *Our Environment: How We Use and Control It.* Allyn and Bacon, New York, 1928.

Cardinal Principles of Secondary Education. Bulletin, 1918, No. 35. U. S. Bureau of Education.

Chemistry for Secondary Schools in Indiana. Bulletin, 1920, No. 26. U. S. Bureau of Education.

Committee Reports. *Chemistry for the High School.* Curriculum Bulletin No. 32, Board of Education, City of St. Louis, 1926.

Course of Study Monograph No. 34. School Publication No. 98. Los Angeles City Schools, June 1924.

Curriculum Revision Committee. *Senior High School Chemistry.* Denver Public Schools, 1927.

Reorganization of Science in Secondary Schools. Bulletin, 1920, No. 26. U. S. Bureau of Education.

Specifications for Standard Arrangement and Equipment of Chemistry Rooms in High Schools of the City of New York. Approved by the Board of Superintendents, June 14, 1926. (Mimeographed copy.)

Specifications for Standard Equipment of General Science Departments in High Schools. Approved by Board of Superintendents, New York City, April 22, 1926. (Mimeographed copy.)

Standard State Lists of High School Laboratory Equipment. Central Scientific Company, Chicago, 1927.

APPENDIX A

SOME SUGGESTED RADIO INSTALLATIONS

The descriptions of installations are limited to the larger items of interest, with the idea in mind of aiding in the choice of kinds of installations best suited to particular needs. No attempt is made to describe all the possible kinds of installations, but rather to describe several kinds at different levels of elaborateness. The order of treatment is from the elaborate to the simple. It is possible to modify any of the individual kinds of installations described below and to combine several kinds. Those details which must be considered when the general kind of installation has been determined are given in Chapter III.

Installation Number 1

This type of installation is intended for school systems where extensive use is to be made of radio in educational work.

Each building shall be provided with a centralized audio frequency distribution system. This system shall have facilities for picking up signals, amplifying them, and distributing them at audio frequencies (those frequencies to which the ear is sensitive) to loud speakers located in all the classrooms, the principal's office, the operator's room, the auditorium, the cafeteria, the open air theater, and any other places to be covered. The loud speakers inside the building shall be permanently located. Portable loud speakers shall be used at outside locations.

The radio receiver equipment shall be capable of picking up radio programs transmitted either through the air or over wires. Both short and long wave reception shall be provided for.

Such broadcasting microphone equipment shall be furnished as will permit picking up announcements from the principal's office as well as speech and music from the auditorium and other broadcasting stations within the building or on the school grounds. In places where large groups present programs several microphones shall be provided. These microphones shall be connected to a mixing panel so that the signals transmitted by the individual microphone can be blended to give a satisfactory combined effect. In auditoriums the mixing panel shall be located on the stage or in the motion picture projection booth. In order to care for situations where parts of a program are to be given from places widely separated from each other, provisions shall be made for connecting the microphones located at these places with a control panel where the operator may connect any microphone with the amplifying and distributing system. This arrangement is especially convenient for broadcasting programs from a banquet room where speakers are seated some distance apart.

Phonograph turntables, pickups, and associated equipment shall be provided for impressing upon the system music and speech reproduced from phonograph records.

The auditorium shall be equipped with microphones and loud speakers so that a speaker on the stage can be heard distinctly by a person with normal hearing, stationed at any place in the room. Similar provisions shall be made for covering outdoor theaters and stadiums.

The central station and all the central station equipment shall be located near the principal's office, preferably in an adjoining room. The control panel may be located in the principal's office. Provision shall be made for the principal or the central station operator to connect, by means of switches, any individual loud speakers, groups of loud speakers, or all the loud speakers to the amplifying system for the reproduction of programs. In short, the principal shall have complete supervision of all the programs being reproduced by each loud speaker associated with the central station in that building. The central station shall be connected by telephone with all rooms and out-of-door stations where loud speakers are located so that reports can be received from these places while the program is being reproduced. As a further check on program reproduction, the principal and the central station operator shall have monitoring loud speakers which can be connected with any desired output circuit from the amplifiers. Adequate provision shall be made in the matter of volume controls located at the central station and in the rooms which have loud speakers. Such amplifying equipment as will permit using radio receivers, microphones, and phonograph pickup simultaneously for distributing programs to different loud speakers in the building shall be furnished.

In the central station of each building provision shall be made for impressing the programs originating in that building on wires which lead to other buildings in the school system. These programs shall be transmitted at audio frequencies at sufficiently high power levels to be detected and distributed satisfactorily in all the school buildings within the school system which are equipped with audio frequency distribution systems. Each building shall be connected by telephone with every other building in the system so that communication regarding programs can be maintained. The proper switching arrangement shall be provided at the central station in each building so that each station can be made either the receiver or the transmitter of programs.

One centrally located building shall be made a key station. This station shall be equipped so that it can serve as either a transmitting or a receiving station. It shall have facilities for interconnecting the circuits from the different school buildings so that transmitting over the school system's wires can be done from other than the central station when desired. It shall have telephone connections with all other buildings in the school system. The circuits used for the telephones shall not be the same as those used for carrying the broadcasting signals. This key station shall have indicators which show when each outlying station is connected with the school system's broadcasting circuits. It shall have provisions for the use of monitoring loud speakers on the circuits leading to the various schools as well as those within the building where the key station is located. It shall have in addition all the major items of equipment which constitute the set-up of the centralized audio frequency system for any individual school building.

This central or key station shall be located in a school building which is readily accessible, preferably the same building which houses the offices of the superintendent and the supervisory staff. There shall be a regular broadcasting room properly draped and a reception room for the performers. All broadcasting through and from the central station shall be at audio frequencies. Provisions shall be made for transmitting two simultaneous programs over the wires connecting the different schools. Each school shall be equipped to distribute three programs simultaneously within the building.

This system is essentially a centralized audio frequency distribution system which serves a number of buildings each equipped with its own audio frequency distribution system. With an arrangement of this kind, it is possible to have very close supervision of the use that is made of radio as an aid in education. It is possible to give to every child in the school system or to any desired groups, the best that can be obtained from outside broadcasting stations. Local broadcasting can be planned and carried out in such a way as to coördinate with the school work. Many especially good programs which might otherwise be available for only one school could, under these conditions, be given to a number of schools. The different schools of the system are tied together in a way that is impossible in most situations to-day.

While the system outlined above includes all the schools within a given school system, it will probably be advisable, in introducing this type of installation, to start with a small group of schools of the same kind, like several elementary schools, or several high schools.

Installation Number 2

The installation shall provide for a complete audio frequency distribution system within one or more buildings, but there shall be no facilities for wire broadcasting between the buildings. The input services, wiring, and loud speaker locations shall be the same as for Installation Number 1. This installation shall provide for three simultaneous programs or channels. All loud speakers within the building shall be permanently mounted so that every station served will have a loud speaker available at all times. Portable loud speakers shall be used on outside locations.

Installation Number 3

This installation differs from Installation Number 2 in that only one channel shall be provided. Extra wires shall be drawn through the conduit in order that another channel may be added later if desired.

Installation Number 4

This installation is intended for use in old buildings or new ones where, for financial or other reasons, it is impossible to provide a separate system of wiring for distributing the radio programs. The central station equipment shall be the same as for Installation Number 3, with the addition of switches or relays for disconnecting the telephone equipment and connecting the radio equipment and vice versa. The telephone circuits shall be used as the circuits for distributing the radio programs. Relays operated from the central station, or switches for manual operation, shall be installed at the positions where telephones and loud speakers are located. These relays or switches shall provide the means for connecting the telephones or the loud speakers to the circuit as desired. With this arrangement the telephone cannot be used when the loud speakers are in operation.

Another installation which can be used in old buildings is described on the last page of Chapter II. In this installation the program bell circuits are used.

Installation Number 5

The following is a more detailed description of an installation for a school having an auditorium, a gymnasium, and a cafeteria in addition to the regular classrooms.

1. *Central type of system.* The installation shall be such that programs can be impressed on the system at a central station and then distributed at audio frequencies to loud speakers located in all the individual classrooms, the auditorium, cafeteria, gymnasium, or any other positions to be served.

2. *Input equipment.* The central station shall have the following program originating (input) equipment:

   a. Radio receiver with provisions for both short and long wave reception.

   b. Broadcasting microphone.

   c. Phonograph pickup.

   d. Provisions for picking up audio frequencies from wires, such as the incoming telephone lines.

The associated apparatus shall be designed so that the change from one kind of program input to another can be accomplished by operating switches.

3. *Interschool transmission and reception of programs.* Such provisions shall be made as will permit (1) the transmitting at audio frequencies over wires to other buildings programs which originate in this building, and (2) the receiving over wires and the distributing to classrooms in this building of the programs which originate in other buildings.

4. *Principal's supervision of programs.*

   a. A controlled device shall be installed at the central station which will enable the principal to connect any loud speaker, group of loud speakers, or all the loud speakers to the amplifying equipment.

b. Volume control equipment for each loud speaker circuit shall be a part of the central station equipment. These volume controls shall be in addition to the volume controls which are located near the loud speaker outlets.

c. Indicating instruments shall be installed at the central station to give a visual indication of the amount of power which is being supplied to each loud speaker circuit, as well as to show when undesirable distortion is taking place. One instrument may be used provided there are adequate switching provisions for testing each loud speaker circuit.

d. In addition to the instrument mentioned in *c*, each central station shall have a monitoring loud speaker which can be connected with each loud speaker circuit to give an auditory check on the output into that circuit.

e. The controls over all the electric power supplied to the system shall be located at the central station where they are easily accessible to the principal.

5. *Location of central station equipment.* The central station equipment shall be placed in the principal's office or in an adjoining room.

6. *Electric power supply.* The major part of the electric power supply to this equipment shall be obtained from the same source of electric power which serves the lighting circuits in the building. It shall be permissible to supply the electric power for the broadcasting microphones from storage batteries. The storage cells shall be the lead-sulphuric acid type. Bulb chargers shall be used for charging the storage batteries.

7. *Central station racks and panels.* There shall be a separate rack for each channel or simultaneous program. The present installation shall provide for one channel. The steel framework of the rack shall be bolted to the floor. The rack shall be designed so that duplicate panels can be added. Fire-resistive material should be used. Meters, switches, input equipment, amplifiers, and other equipment mounted on the rack shall be protected adequately from dust and accidental injury.

8. *Amplifier equipment.* The amplifier equipment shall be such that the signals from the input equipment can be amplified sufficiently to be reproduced satisfactorily by every loud speaker in the system. Facilities shall be furnished for varying the energy output from the amplifying system.

9. *Circuits to loud speakers.* The circuits from the central station to the loud speakers in the rooms shall be run in regular iron conduit. Four wires shall connect each loud speaker location with the central station. In the present installation only two of these wires will be in service where the circuits run to magnetic loud speakers. The extra pair of wires shall be retained as spares for future addition of another channel. In circuits where dynamic loud speakers are employed, all four wires shall be in service; two for signals and two for magnetic field power supply. The circuit shall be installed so that there will be no destructive induction or capacity effects between circuits.

10. *Classroom loud speakers.* The loud speakers installed in the classrooms shall be of the magnetic type. These loud speakers shall be located

in the front corner of the room on the side toward the corridor. A volume control shall be associated with each loud speaker and shall be so located that the teacher can reach it easily. The volume output from the class-room loud speaker shall be at such a level that the programs can be heard easily in all parts of the room. The loud speakers shall be mounted flush with the wall.

11. *Auditorium loud speaker.* The auditorium loud speaker shall be of the dynamic type. The installation shall be such that programs can be heard distinctly in all parts of the room. The number of loud speakers necessary shall be determined by the size and acoustic properties of the room. Where microphones are to be used in the same room with the loud speakers, the microphones shall be placed sufficiently far behind the loud speakers to prevent interference between the units.

12. *Loud speakers for cafeteria.* Dynamic loud speakers shall be used in the cafeteria. These loud speakers shall be located so that programs can be heard distinctly in all parts of the room and so that the sound emitted by these loud speakers will not produce disturbing effects in adjoining classrooms.

13. *Loud speakers for gymnasium.* Dynamic loud speakers shall be used in the gymnasium. These loud speakers shall be located in positions which are not hazardous; for instance on side walls, out of the direct line of play. In buildings where the gymnasium and a dressing room adjoin, the loud speaker shall be placed in the separating wall provided this location is satisfactory where acoustic properties of the room are concerned. In all cases the loud speakers shall be properly located to minimize the conduc-tion of sound into classrooms.

14. *Loud speakers mounted permanently.* All loud speakers shall be so mounted that they cannot be moved from place to place. Portable loud speakers shall not be used in any part of the installation.

15. *Location of microphone outlets.* Microphone outlets shall be pro-vided in the principal's office, in the auditorium, and in any other room which is to be used as a broadcasting studio. Provision shall be made for the use of several microphones in the auditorium. Where several micro-phones are used to pick up the same program, their outputs shall be fed into a mixing panel. The mixing panel shall have facilities for regulating the output from the several microphones so that the total effect will be blended properly. Portable two-button carbon microphones shall be used.

16. *Antenna.* An inverted L type outdoor antenna shall be furnished. The lead-in from this antenna shall be brought down along the outside of the building to the central station, or, if brought down on the inside of the building, it shall be inside fibre conduit. No conduit is to be used for a lead-in brought down on the outside of the building. The antenna equipment shall include a loop aërial, also to be used in the central station.

17. *Vacuum tubes.* Vacuum tubes shall be furnished for all positions in which they are needed. There shall be supplied, in addition, one reserve tube of each type used in the installation.

18. *Testing.* Provision shall be made for testing each individual circuit

separately without interfering in any way with any of the other circuits. The necessary testing equipment shall be furnished as a part of the installation.

19. *Instruction.* The installing engineers shall instruct the principal or some person designated by him concerning the operation and care of the equipment.

20. *Service.* The installing contractor shall arrange for the servicing of the equipment for a period of at least one year after installation.

21. *Materials used.* Materials used in the installation shall meet the standard requirements of such organizations as American Society for Testing Materials, American Society of Mechanical Engineers, American Institute of Electrical Engineers, Radio Manufacturing Association, Electric Power Club, and American Specifications Institute.

22. *Local and other regulations.* The installation shall conform in every respect to the rules and regulations of local and other organizations having jurisdiction over this type of installation.

APPENDIX B

RECOMMENDATIONS—ELECTRIC POWER SUPPLY INSTALLATIONS

The following recommendations are made in four groups according to the elaborateness of the facilities provided. The facilities recommended in any of the groups are ample to meet the needs determined in this study. The numerical values given for machine rating and the like should be considered as representing general levels and not specific values. For important considerations in the choice and installation of panel boards and panel board equipment see Appendix C. It is assumed that the power supply for lighting and the like is AC. If this is not the case, the AC supply to the master panel shall be obtained from motor-generator sets or rotary converters.

PHYSICS

Group A. The following recommendations are particularly applicable to situations in which it is desired that pupils shall be given considerable laboratory experience. Fixed tables are to be used in the laboratory. This equipment is to supply no power to other science laboratories.

1. The physics department shall have one laboratory used for laboratory work only, a lecture-room, a combination shop and storeroom, a dark room, and one or more recitation rooms. The dark room and the shop shall be between the laboratory and the lecture-room. The recitation rooms need not connect with the other rooms but shall be near them.
2. A master panel (control board) shall be located in the physics shop, a resistance panel in the lecture-room and a distribution panel in the laboratory.
3. The following shall be supplied to the master panel board: (*a*) single-phase 110 volts AC, 50 ampere capacity from the city supply; (*b*) three-phase 220 volts AC, 20 ampere capacity from the city supply; (*c*) 110 volts DC, 50 ampere capacity from the motor generator; and (*d*) 24 volts DC from 75 ampere-hour storage battery.
4. The storage battery shall be made up of 75 ampere-hour capacity cells. The total battery voltage shall be 24. The battery shall be set on a rack in the physics shop. A Number 10 copper wire shall be run from each cell of the battery to the master panel. Either nickel-iron-alkaline cells or lead-sulphuric acid cells may be used. The lead-sulphuric acid cells shall be of a sealed type with glass jars.
5. The motor-generator set shall consist of a seven and one-half horse-

172

power motor and a five and five-eighths kilowatt 125 volt direct current generator, both mounted on a single metal base which in turn is mounted on a hardwood base and a one and one-fourth inch layer of best compressed cork. The entire unit is to be bolted to the floor in the physics shop. Jamb nuts are to be used on the bolts which extend through the layer of cork.

6. The battery panel shall have (a) DC ammeter, (b) DC voltmeter and test key, (c) bulb rectifier with transformer on back of panel, (d) charging switch, (e) battery charging rheostat with scale so that any section of the battery can be charged at the correct rate, (f) jacks or other contacts for various battery taps to connect any section of the battery to the charging circuits, (g) jacks or other contacts for connecting any section of the battery with the voltmeter, and (h) fuses. Switchboard wattmeters and watt-hour meters are desirable but not necessary.

7. A control panel shall be a part of the master panel. The equipment on this control panel shall be (a) starting compensator for the motor, (b) field rheostat for the generator, (c) DC voltmeter, (d) DC ammeter, and (e) circuit breakers or fuses. Copper wire not smaller than Number 6 shall be used in the feeder circuit from the control panel to the jack or distribution panel of the master panel.

8. A transformer of one kilowatt capacity shall be made a permanent part of the master panel equipment. The primary shall be connected to the 110 volt AC supply and taps shall be taken from the secondary so as to supply AC in four volt steps from four to twenty-four. These taps are to be connected with jacks or other contacts in order to make possible the distribution of this current at the various voltage levels to any outlets desired.

9. The three-phase 220 volt AC shall be brought to the master panel so that connections can be made with either of the three phases as desired.

10. Single conductor flexible cords with side opening lugs or special insertion plugs on both ends shall be furnished as a part of the master panel equipment to connect the various current supply circuits with the outlying station circuits which terminate on the master panel. Number 6 and Number 10 gauge stage cable or other reinforced copper wires shall be used for this purpose.

11. Circuits from the following outlying outlets and panels shall terminate at the master panel: (a) one 50 ampere capacity outlet in the rear wall of the lecture-room; (b) one 50 ampere capacity outlet and two 30 ampere capacity outlets on the demonstration table in the laboratory and also in the lecture-room; (c) one 50 and one 30 ampere capacity outlet in the recitation room; (d) one 30 and one 10 ampere capacity outlet in the physics shop; (e) distribution panel in the laboratory, three circuits; and (f) one 10 ampere capacity outlet in the dark room. The circuits to the 50 ampere capacity outlets and to the distribution panel in the laboratory shall be of Number 6 B and S gauge copper wire.

12. The physics laboratory distribution panel shall have the following

equipment: (*a*) knife switches or heavy duty snap switches for each circuit from the master panel board; (*b*) a jack or a wing nut connection as a terminal for each wire of each circuit from the master panel and like terminals for the circuits from the pupils' tables and the demonstration table; (*c*) flexible, rubber-covered conductors, Number 12 gauge, with lugs or plug terminals for connecting supply circuits with table circuits; and (*d*) fuses for all circuits. The distribution panel shall be placed at some convenient place near the front of the room.

13. There shall be one table electric outlet for each pupil station in the laboratory. Each table outlet shall be connected with the laboratory distribution panel by a separate pair of Number 14 gauge copper wires. One of the circuits to the laboratory demonstration table shall be connected with the distribution board.

14. The lecture-room resistance panel shall have the following equipment: (*a*) two grid resistances with dial switch control, one in the circuit with the 50 ampere outlet and the other with a 30 ampere outlet on the demonstration table; (*b*) two illuminated type voltmeters with multiples, one for DC and the other for AC; (*c*) two illuminated type ammeters with shunts, one for DC and the other for AC; (*d*) one 50 ampere capacity knife switch for the circuit to the 50 ampere outlet on the demonstration table; (*e*) one 25 ampere capacity switch for the circuit to the 30 ampere capacity outlet on the demonstration table; and (*f*) one 25 ampere double throw switch for the circuit from the master panel to an outlet on the table, arranged on one side to supply current to the outlet and on the other side to supply current from the outlet through the ammeter. The resistance panel shall be placed behind and to one side of the demonstration table.

Group B. The following recommendations are intended for schools where the lecture-room is used by all the science departments; where considerable emphasis is placed upon individual laboratory work; and where the classes are comparatively large.

1. The physics department shall have one laboratory, a combination shop and storeroom, a lecture-room shared with other science departments, and a dark room. The shop and dark room shall be located between the laboratory and the lecture-room.

2. A master panel (control board) shall be arranged to set flush into the wall between the laboratory and the shop. The front of the panel shall be covered by glass doors which open into the laboratory. The back of the panel shall be covered by steel doors which open into the shop.

3. The following shall be supplied to the master panel: (*a*) single-phase 110 volt AC, 20 amperes capacity, from the city supply; (*b*) 110 volts DC, 20 ampere capacity, from a motor-generator set; and (*c*) twenty-four volts DC, from 50 ampere-hour storage battery.

4. The requirements for the storage battery equipment including the panel and the charging equipment shall be the same as given above in paragraphs four and five, Group A, except that 50 ampere-hour capacity cells shall be used.

5. The motor-generator set shall consist of a two kilowatt 125 volt DC generator and a three and one-half horsepower motor. The method of mounting the control equipment shall be similar to that given above in paragraphs 6 and 7 of Group A.
6. The transformer mounted on the master panel board shall be one-half kilowatt capacity with taps to give 6-12-24 volts AC. Provisions for distribution shall be the same as those given above in paragraph 8 of Group A.
7. The manner of interconnecting circuits shall be like that described in paragraph 10 of Group A, except that Number 10 A.W.G. reinforced flexible cord shall be used throughout.
8. The distribution circuits to be run from the master panel are as follows: (*a*) circuits to pupils' tables in the physics laboratory, one for every two pupil stations; (*b*) three circuits to the demonstration table in the physics laboratory; (*c*) three circuits to the demonstration table in the lecture-room; (*d*) one circuit to the physics dark room; (*e*) two circuits to the demonstration table in each biology room and each science room; (*f*) two circuits to the distribution panel in each chemistry laboratory; and (*g*) one circuit to the physics shop. All circuits shall be either Number 10 or Number 12 A.W.G. wire, preferably Number 10.
9. The distribution panel section of the master panel shall be provided with a jack or a wing-nut connector as a terminal for each wire of each current supply circuit and like terminals for all of the circuits mentioned in paragraph 8 of this group.
10. The lecture-room resistance panel shall have equipment similar to that described in paragraph 14 of Group A, except that the maximum ampere capacity of the switches and the resistances shall be twenty-five.
11. Twenty-ampere capacity wall outlets shall be placed in the following places: (*a*) one in the rear of the lecture-room; (*b*) one near a window in the shop; and (*c*) one near the sink in the dark room. These wall outlets shall be connected with the lighting panel.

Group C. The following recommendations are intended for a school where the same room is used for the laboratory work demonstrations and recitations.

1. The physics department shall have one combination laboratory and recitation room, a dark room, and a combination shop and storeroom. Fixed pupils' tables shall be used. The teacher's demonstration table shall be located near the wall which separates the physics shop from the main physics room.
2. The master panel board shall be set flush into the wall between the laboratory and the shop. The front of the panel board shall be accessible from the laboratory, and the rear of the board shall be accessible from the shop. Both the front and the back of the panel board shall be protected by doors.
3. This master panel board shall include the distribution panel, the panel for the motor generator, and the panel for the storage battery and charging equipment.

4. The equipment shall be the same as described in Group B with the following exceptions: (*a*) a twelve volt, thirty ampere-hour storage battery shall be used; (*b*) the motor-generator set shall furnish one kilowatt DC, at 110 volts; and (*c*) the lecture-room resistance panel shall be omitted.

Group D. The following recommendations are intended for a school where the permanent wiring is to be reduced to a minimum. The following installation facilities change the room from a science laboratory to a regular recitation room. Some conveniences are sacrificed for economy.

1. There shall be one combination laboratory and recitation room, and one combination shop and storeroom. The teacher's demonstration table shall be permanently located. All the pupils' tables shall be movable.
2. A fourteen-inch shelf shall be built along the outside wall and along the wall which separates the laboratory from the corridor. This shelf shall be approximately thirty inches above the floor.
3. Gas outlets and electric outlets for pupils' use shall protrude through the shelf at points near the wall. All piping shall be run immediately below the shelf.
4. Outlets shall be provided at intervals of three feet throughout the length of each shelf. At each outlet position along a shelf there shall be two outlets. One outlet of each pair is on one circuit and the other on another circuit. The two circuits shall be run in separate conduits. There shall be four wall circuits for pupils' use, two along the outside wall and two along the corridor wall. All the outlets on any one circuit shall be in parallel. There shall be three additional outlets, each on its own circuit, two on the teacher's demonstration table and one near the work table in the shop.
5. All the circuits mentioned above shall terminate on a panel. This panel shall be located in the shop.
6. Provisions shall be made on the panel board so that any current supply available can be connected with circuits to the tables. The circuit to the pupils' outlets shall be either Number 10 or Number 12 A.W.G. wire.
7. The following current supplies shall be available: (*a*) 110 volt single-phase AC from the lighting panel, (*b*) 70 to 125 volts DC from a 750 watt motor generator, (*c*) six volts DC from a 30 ampere-hour storage battery, (*d*) dry cells, (*e*) one-half kilowatt transformer to give 6, 12, and 24 volts AC.
8. Portable storage batteries shall be used. Bulb rectifiers shall be used for charging. Other low voltage DC shall be obtained from dry cells.
9. A 750 watt motor-generator set capable of producing DC at 90 to 125 volts. The motor-generator set, along with its meters and starting and control equipment, shall be mounted on a truck so that the entire outfit can be moved about at will.
10. Each of the outlets on the circuits which connect with the panel board shall be fused. All feeder circuits shall be fused.
11. One extra 20 ampere capacity wall outlet shall be provided in each of

the following places: (*a*) storeroom and shop, (*b*) rear of the laboratory, (*c*) on the teacher's demonstration table.
12. Dry rectifiers such as those used in radio may be used for DC supplies where the amperage requirements are small.

CHEMISTRY

Group A. These recommendations are intended for a very large school where much emphasis is placed upon industrial chemistry, particularly the electrical process. This installation is more elaborate than is necessary for a school where only the usual courses in high school chemistry are taught.
1. The following rooms in the department shall be supplied with electric power from the master panel: laboratories, lecture and recitation rooms, and preparation room.
2. A master panel shall be located in the preparation room, a resistance panel in each lecture-room, and a distribution panel in each laboratory.
3. The equipment shall be exactly the same as that described under Group A of physics installations. The power supplies for the chemistry department shall be entirely independent of those for any other science department.
Group B. The following recommendations are intended for a school where individual laboratory work is emphasized but where the demands for electric power are not sufficient to warrant having a motor-generator set, storage battery equipment, etc., for the use of the chemistry department alone.
1. The following shall be obtained from the master panel and associated equipment located in the physics shop or other central distribution points: (*a*) direct current at 110 volt level, from motor-generator set; (*b*) direct current at 12 volt level, from storage batteries.
2. The 110 volt AC and 220 volt AC shall be obtained from the house-lighting and power panels.
3. Provisions shall be made so that the generator current and the storage battery current can be obtained by operating switches located on the chemistry sub-panels.
4. The following circuits for distributing power shall connect with the sub-panel in each chemistry laboratory: (*a*) three circuits to the teacher's demonstration table; (*b*) one circuit with two outlets in parallel for each group of four pupil stations; (*c*) one circuit to an outlet in each hood. One of the circuits to the demonstration table shall be of Number 6 wire, the other circuits shall be of Number 10 wire.
5. The laboratory sub-panel shall be supplied with: (*a*) 110 volts AC; (*b*) 220 volts AC; (*c*) 110 volts DC; and (*d*) 12 volts DC. Nothing smaller than Number 10 wire shall be used for these circuits.
6. The chemistry distribution panel shall have facilities similar to those described in paragraph 12 of Group A of recommendations for installation in the physics department.
7. The sub-panel in each chemistry lecture or recitation room shall be like

the chemistry laboratory sub-panel in all respects except that there shall be no circuits to pupils' tables.

8. One of the outlets provided in the preparation room shall be connected with the nearest lecture-room sub-panel or a laboratory sub-panel. Two other outlets in the preparation room shall be connected with the lighting panel.

9. One 20 ampere capacity outlet shall be provided in the rear wall or in a side wall, well to the rear of each lecture or recitation room. These outlets shall be connected with the lighting circuit.

10. One 6 volt 80 ampere-hour capacity storage battery may be used in place of the storage battery supply from the central station.

Group C. The following recommendations are intended for a school where the pupils' chemistry experiments require little or no electricity and where the laboratory experiments and recitation work are to be carried on in the same room.

1. Electric power shall be supplied to a panel and then distributed to the demonstration table outlets, outlets on the pupils' tables, (if any are used) and outlets in the chemistry preparation room.

2. The teacher's demonstration table shall be provided with four outlets. One of these outlets shall be 30 amperes capacity, the others 20 amperes capacity. These outlets shall be connected with the distribution panel.

3. The chemistry sub-panel shall be supplied with the following: (*a*) 110 volt AC from the lighting panel; (*b*) 220 volt AC from the power panel; (*c*) 110 volt DC from the master panel; and (*d*) 12 volt DC from the master panel.

4. One or two 6 volt 30 ampere-hour capacity portable storage batteries may be used instead of the battery supply from the master panel. If the course is planned so that only small amperage DC is required at low voltages, dry cells may be used for this supply.

5. Provisions shall be made for connecting the 220 AC supply with the 30 ampere capacity outlet on the teacher's demonstration table. This service is planned for use with a transformer to supply current for large wattage electric furnaces.

6. One 10 ampere capacity outlet shall be provided for every two pupil stations. These outlets shall be on circuits which are connected with the chemistry sub-panel. All the outlets on pupils' tables may be omitted if the pupils' experiments require the use of dry cells only.

7. There shall be two outlets in the preparation room, one connected with the sub-panel and the other with the lighting panel.

8. The chemistry distribution panel shall have facilities similar to those described in paragraph 12 of Group A, recommendations for a physics department installation.

9. One 20 ampere outlet shall be located in each hood. These outlets shall be connected with the distribution panel. They shall be designed to withstand the action of fumes.

Biology

Group A. The following recommendations are intended for a school having several biology recitation rooms, several laboratories, a preparation room and a storeroom.

1. No electric outlets shall be provided on the pupils' tables.
2. One 10 ampere and one 30 ampere capacity outlet shall be located on the demonstration table of each recitation room and each laboratory. The 30 ampere outlet shall be controlled by a two-way switch. One side of the switch shall be connected with a circuit to the nearest master panel in the science department and the other side with a circuit connected with the lighting panel. The 10 ampere outlet and both circuits to the master panel may be omitted if dry cells or portable storage cells are to be used for the DC supply.
3. One 20 ampere wall outlet shall be located at the rear of each recitation room and each laboratory. Two 10 ampere wall outlets shall be provided in the preparation room. These outlets shall be connected with the lighting panel.
4. The ampere capacity of each circuit should be clearly marked on the outlet which it supplies. Those circuits which supply current from the lighting panel shall be marked 110 volts AC. The polarity shall be indicated on those outlets which are on circuits connected with the master panel.
5. Several 10 ampere capacity wall outlets shall be placed at convenient locations in the laboratory for use with sterilizers and microscope illuminators. These outlets shall be connected with the lighting panel.

Group B. The following recommendations are intended for a biology department where little electricity is used for experimental purposes, and where none of the projection machines require more than 10 or 15 amperes.

1. No electric outlets shall be located on the pupils' tables.
2. One 20 ampere capacity outlet shall be located on the teacher's demonstration table in each laboratory and each recitation room.
3. Twenty ampere capacity outlets shall be located as follows: (*a*) one on the teacher's demonstration table in each laboratory and recitation room; (*b*) one wall outlet near the rear of each recitation room and each laboratory. These outlets shall be connected with the lighting panel.
4. Ten ampere capacity wall outlets shall be located as follows: (*a*) two in the preparation room, one over the work table, and the other above the sterilizer wall table; (*b*) two in each laboratory in the side wall toward the corridor. These outlets shall be supplied with current from the lighting panel.
5. If the laboratory work and the recitations are conducted in the same room, the recommendations made above for the laboratory shall apply to the combination laboratory-recitation rooms.
6. All the direct current supply shall be obtained from Number 6 dry cells or from a six volt 30 ampere-hour storage battery.

GENERAL SCIENCE

Group A. These recommendations are made for a school in which it is intended that pupils shall be allowed individual laboratory work with considerable use of electricity.

1. Circuits of 20 ampere capacity shall connect the master panel for the science departments with the following: (*a*) one distribution panel in each laboratory; (*b*) two outlets on the teacher's demonstration table in each recitation room; (*c*) one outlet in the wall near the work table in the preparation room. The circuits shall be connected with the nearest master panel if there are several master panels in the science departments.

2. Circuits of 20 amperes capacity shall connect the lighting panel with the following: (*a*) distribution panel in each laboratory; (*b*) one outlet on the teacher's demonstration table in each recitation room; and (*c*) one outlet in the wall at the rear of each laboratory and each recitation room.

3. The distribution panel in each laboratory shall be supplied with AC and DC generator current at approximately 110 volt level, and storage battery current at approximately 24 volt level.

4. This distribution of panels in the laboratories shall be the means of controlling the current supply to the pupils' tables and the teacher's demonstration table in the laboratory.

5. The biology laboratory distribution panel shall have facilities similar to those described in paragraph 12 of Group A, recommendations for a physics department installation.

6. Provide one outlet at each pupil station in the laboratory. There shall be one circuit for each three or four outlets. The circuits shall be arranged to require the minimum amount of wiring. Either Number 14 or Number 12 A.W.G. wires shall be used in these circuits. All the circuits shall terminate at the laboratory distribution board.

7. All circuits and outlets shall be marked accurately and clearly. Outlets on circuits to pupils' tables, teacher's demonstration table and all circuits to the master panels shall have the polarity indicated.

8. A large dial DC ammeter and a large dial DC voltmeter shall be mounted on the wall behind the demonstration table in each recitation room. Each meter shall be connected with an outlet on the demonstration table. The ammeter shall be provided with shunts to give full scale readings on 3 and 30 amperes. The voltmeter shall have multipliers to give full scale readings on one and one-half, fifteen, and 150 volts.

Group B. These recommendations are intended for a general science department where the laboratory work and the demonstration work are carried on in the same room and where the pupils perform few experiments which require the use of electricity.

1. There shall be one 10 ampere capacity outlet for each pupil station in the laboratory. All of these outlets shall be on the same circuit.

This circuit shall terminate on a distribution panel located near the teacher's demonstration table.

2. The distribution panel shall have facilities for connecting the pupil's table circuit and the circuits from the demonstration table with the various current supplies. The fuses for all the circuits shall be located on the distribution panel.

3. Current shall be supplied to the distribution panel by three circuits— two connected with the master panel and one connected with the lighting panel. Generator DC at 110 volt levels and storage battery current at 12 or 24 volt levels shall be obtained from the master panel. The circuit to the lighting panel shall supply AC at 110 volt levels. It shall be permissible to obtain the low voltage DC from portable storage batteries or dry cells, particularly if the master panel and its associated equipment are far from the general science rooms.

4. The provisions for meters and meter circuits shall be like those described in paragraph 8 of Group A, recommendations for general science.

5. There shall be three circuits connecting outlets on the teacher's demonstration table with the distribution panel.

6. One outlet in the preparation room shall be connected with the master panel, and another connected with the lighting panel. The outlets shall be located near the work table.

7. Two 20 ampere capacity wall outlets shall be located in the laboratory, one at the rear of the room, and the other near the teacher's table. These outlets shall be connected with the lighting panel.

8. It shall be permissible to use a portable motor-generator set as the source of direct current supply. This unit shall be mounted on a small truck. It shall be capable of delivering 750 watts.

Group C. These recommendations shall be the same as those given in Group D of the recommendations for the electric supply installations for a physics department.

TYPICAL SPECIFICATIONS

The following specifications were prepared by Mr. Joe A. Kavanagh, The Holtzer-Cabot Electric Company, to meet the requirements placed by the author.

Scope.

The contractor shall furnish and install complete, at locations shown on the floor plan, one main laboratory distributing board, one lecturers' meter and resistance unit in lecture-room and (—) sub-panels. The main distributing board shall be arranged for the proper control of AC and DC voltages and designed so that any voltage on the board may be metered and protected by circuit breakers and transferred by means of plug and jack connections over tie lines to any or all sub-panels.

All equipment shall be of the design originated and set forth as a standard by The Holtzer-Cabot Electric Company for laboratory practice, i.e., equipment shall be of the dead front construction and designed so that no live parts shall be exposed to the hands of the students or instructors.

Main Laboratory Distributing Board.

This board shall consist of seven unit panels mounted over a steel, wall case. These panels shall be made of ⅛" pressed steel, formed back one inch on all four sides, ground smooth, sand blasted, and covered with a hard, black, eggshell finish. This board shall consist of the following unit panels:

One panel for the control of outgoing circuits. It shall have the proper number of two- and three-wire jacks properly designated by engraved name plates. Each circuit of jacks shall be so designed that it is removable from the front of the panel and protected from the other jacks by a barrier, so that these wires are encased separately from one another from the jack terminal to the conduit entrance in the box. This panel is to be equal to Holtzer-Cabot K-165-F-165.

One panel unit for the control of battery voltages with the proper number of jacks for battery voltage taps equipped with circuit breaker for each tap, one voltmeter and ammeter with plug connections, one rectifier with control switch and indicator, and one rheostat. Plugs on this panel shall be arranged so that any cell or group of cells may be charged individually. This panel is to be equal to Holtzer-Cabot K 164-240.

One panel unit shall be typical to panel #2 except that this will be equipped with a transformer with voltage taps and will have no rectifier. This panel is to be equal to Holtzer-Cabot K-165-160.

One panel unit shall be for the control of the motor-generator set and shall have mounted thereon control apparatus, field rheostat, and relay with red pilot lights. This panel is to be equal to Holtzer-Cabot K-165-15.

One panel unit for the control of 110 volts DC with associated meters, circuit breaker, jack connections, etc. This panel is to be equal to Holtzer-Cabot 165-130.

One panel unit for the control of 110 volt single phase with meters, circuit breakers, jack connections, etc. This panel is to be equal to Holtzer-Cabot K-165-130.

One panel unit for the control of 220 volt, three-phase, with associated meters, circuit breakers, jack connections, etc. This panel is to be of the dead front type equal to Holtzer-Cabot K-165-3P.

The above panel units are to be flush type, i.e., all meters, circuit breakers, etc., on this panel shall be flush with the face of the panel.

Transferring Equipment.

All panels shall have the proper number of plugs and jacks mounted in bakelite shells, for transferring the different voltages to outgoing lines. The jacks and plugs shall be of two different types as a precaution against setting up wrong connections, the contact part shall be cut out of solid brass and designed to keep a permanent tension and self-cleaning contact at all times.

The portable plugs and jacks shall be of the same design and shall be connected by a stranded rubber Tirex cord, of the proper A.W.G. for the current they are to carry.

Sub-Panels.

Where sub-panels are used they also shall be of the flush construction mounted over wall case extended through the wall and having hinged door and Yale lock on the opposite side of the wall. These panels shall be equipped with plug and jack connections going to the students' tables in the laboratory which the panel is to take care of, and shall also have tie lines connected to the main distributing panel. This sub-panel board shall have mounted thereon one AC volt and ammeter one DC volt and ammeter and a circuit breaker for each students' table outlet associated with its jack connections. These panels are to be equal to H.C. 165-7.

Lecture-Room.

The contractor shall furnish and install at a location over the blackboard in the lecture-room the unit meter panels consisting of the following meters:

1 AC voltmeter:	0–150.	H.C.	Laboratory type or equal.
2 AC ammeters:	0– 30.	"	" " " "
1 DC voltmeter:	0–150.	"	" " " "
1 DC ammeter:	0– 30.	"	" " " "
1 AC ammeter:	0– 5.	"	" " " "
1 AC voltmeter:	0– 60.	"	" " " "
1 DC ammeter:	0– 5.		

Directly below the blackboard the contractor shall furnish load resistance units consisting of two resistance panels and one plug and jack panel for the control of the circuit to the instructor's desk; for the control of the loading resistance; and for the control of the meters.

Storage Battery.

Furnish and install near the main distributing board one battery consisting of 12 cells of (—) ampere-hour capacity of chloride accumulator, with glass jars and glass sand trays. This battery shall be mounted on a lead covered battery shelf 42 inches from the finished floor lines. Battery and shelf should be equal to H.C. FA-210.

Motor Generator.

Furnish and install near the main distributing board one (—) KW motor-generator set mounted on a cast iron base with a two-inch cork mat. This set shall consist of a three-phase AC motor. The motor shall be coupled to a 2 KW compound-wound direct current generator with field regulation.
This set shall be mounted on a 12-inch concrete foundation.

Conduit Work.

The contractor shall confer with the manufacturer as to the exact point at which the conduits are to enter the switchboard, sub-panel, rheostat units, meter units, etc., and submit detailed drawings to the architect for his approval.

APPENDIX C

SOME IMPORTANT CONSIDERATIONS IN THE CHOICE AND INSTALLATION OF LABORATORY PANEL BOARDS

Safety.

"Live" front boards shall be protected by a door, preferably with glass panels, to cover all exposed switches and circuits. The rear of the board shall be covered with a full opening door. If the panel board is set away from the wall and not enclosed in a box, wire grill should be used to enclose the space between the board and the wall. From the standpoint of safety to the operator, "dead" front boards are more desirable than "live" front boards.

Adaptable to Study Purposes.

The arrangement of the equipment on the panels and the location of the panels and allied equipment should be such as to facilitate their use for study purposes.

Simple to Operate.

Panel boards should be designed so that persons who are not highly trained technicians can operate the equipment satisfactorily.

Flexible Cords.

Stage cable or other heavy reinforced cord should be used for making temporary connections.

Panel Supports.

Panels should be set on angle iron frames or one and one-fourth inch iron pipes and brackets unless they are part of a cabinet or are mounted flush with the wall.

Fire Resistance.

Frames, panels, and coverings for wires back of the board should be fire resistive. Each "live" conductor should be taped with a layer of approved asbestos tape, unless approved asbestos covers surround each wire.

Fuses and Circuit Breakers.

All circuits shall be fused adequately. Circuit breakers should be provided for the motor-generator sets. All other feeder circuits shall be protected with circuit breakers or fuses. Each table circuit shall be fused at the panel board.

Marking.

Panel boards should be marked adequately and clearly. Name plates for all circuits, switches, outlets, etc., should be located permanently in their proper places on the panel board. In addition to the usual markings found on the switchboards, each fuse location should have markings designating the proper fuses to be used. These name plates may be brass or copper properly engraved; rubber or bakelite with engraved letters filled with white enamel and then baked; or inverse etched name plates having raised silvered letters on a black background. The polarity should be indicated on outlets which furnish DC.

Wiring Diagrams and Instructions.

Complete wiring of the equipment as well as instructions for operation should be placed near or on the panel board.

Segregation of Services.

Each table circuit and the individual current supplied (AC, DC, battery) should be segregated permanently from the others with adequate barriers.

Panel Board Materials.

Panel boards may be built of natural black Maine Monson slate, special composition asbestos board like Johns-Mansville Ebony Asbestos Compound 1803-X, or ⅛-inch stretcher level steel. Slate boards must be free from flaws and veins and must be thick enough for strength.

Plugs.

Plugs should make good mechanical contact even after long usage. Plugs having a gradual taper or split plugs and receptacles are desirable. No plugs should be used which do not meet the requirements of the National Board of Fire Underwriters. Plugs for the 110 volt circuit should be fastened permanently in pairs to their cords in order to reduce the likelihood of short circuits. Chromium finish on plugs and receptacles is desirable.

Location of Resistances.

Resistances should be located where there is free circulation of air around them, and where heat given off will not mutilate other equipment.

Location of Circuit Breakers.

Circuit breakers should be located, preferably at the top, where arcing will not mutilate other equipment on the board.

Meters.

Provision should be made for switchboard voltmeters with multipliers (resistances) and ammeters with shunts suitable for measuring the voltages and amperages coming to and from the board. Watt meters and watt-hour meters are desirable but not necessary.

Motor-Generator Tests.

The motor and generator should be mounted on one cast-iron base, and this in turn on a hardwood base with a two-inch layer of the best quality compressed cork to act as a vibration absorber. All bolts passing through the flexible median should have jamb nuts.

Starting Compensator and Field Rheostats for Motor Generator.

A starting compensator with under voltage and overload protection for the motor and a "back of the board" type field rheostat for the generator should be supplied with each motor-generator unit.

Storage Battery Rack.

The storage cells should be set in trays, on racks or shelves so constructed as to minimize the chances of the liquid contents spilling on the floor.

Knife Switch Position.

Knife switches should be placed on the panels so that the handle is up when the circuit is closed. When placed in this position the circuit will be open if the handle drops accidentally. Fuses should be "dead" when the switch is open. When the circuits are on the front of the board the switches may be placed horizontally.

Ratings of Switches.

The current density and other ratings of switches should conform to the standards of the American Institute of Electrical Engineers.

Location of the Panel Boards.

The panel boards should be so located that they occupy the minimum of floor space and so that the wire and conduit runs are as short as possible. The back of the panels should be accessible for servicing and study. Some favorite locations for the panel boards are: (1) in the wall between the preparation room (shop) and the laboratory, the front of the board being in the laboratory and the back of the board in the preparation room; (2) in the wall between the lecture-room and laboratory; and (3) in the wall between the laboratory and the corridor, the front of the board being in the laboratory and the back of the board being accessible from the corridor.

Height of Panel Boards.

The height should be such that all equipment can be reached easily. Approximately seven and one-half feet should be the maximum height.

Spare Outlets.

Spare outlets should be provided for future expansion of service.

APPENDIX D

SUMMARY OF CONCLUSIONS AND SUGGESTIONS CONTAINED IN THE REPORT OF THE COUNTY OF KENT (GREAT BRITAIN) INVESTIGATION

The following quotation is given because it presents a rather complete picture of the results of a carefully planned and conducted investigation in the use of radio in education. Anyone contemplating experiments of this kind will find the entire report very valuable.

1. There is a real and persistent demand from teachers for courses of wireless lessons in subjects associated with the ordinary subjects of the curriculum.
2. The type of receiving apparatus (individual sets) used in the experiment is a satisfactory medium for educational transmissions. It is essential that efficient arrangements be made for periodical inspection and for maintenance of the receiving sets. A special enquiry appeared to shew that certain advantages attached to reception by head-phones as compared with reception by loudspeakers. There are, however, certain serious disadvantages.
3. In the opinion of the teachers the broadcast lessons—
   a. Imparted a knowledge of facts;
   b. Stimulated interest in ways which could be definitely observed;
   c. Created impressions as durable as those produced by their ordinary lessons;
   d. Did not encourage inattention;
   e. Were particularly stimulating to clever children;
   f. Supplied views and information which the teachers themselves could not have supplied;
   g. Gave them fresh ideas for lessons;
   h. Interested some parents in the work that their children did in school.
4. All courses were not uniformly successful. Much remains to be done to ensure better cooperation between lecturer, teacher and pupil, and further investigation is required in many directions.
5. Many teachers are convinced that children are emotionally affected by the knowledge that they are listening in company with thousands of other children, particularly on such occasions as Armistice Day.
6. The lecturer should be an expert; have good delivery; possess some of the qualities of a teacher; have had some teaching experience; have some knowledge of the conditions prevailing in the schools of the type to which he is lecturing; and be prepared to study the special problems of wireless teaching.
7. The teacher chosen to take charge of the broadcast lesson should not be out of sympathy with educational broadcasting and should have some knowledge of the subjects treated.
8. Successful broadcast lessons depend on cooperation between teacher and lecturer. Cooperation has grown during the period of the experiment and is growing. For further growth it is essential that the B.B.C. should maintain close touch with the schools.

9. The average age of a listening class should not, as a rule, be below nine years. Every effort should be made to relieve the class from the strain of uninterrupted listening, and to induce individual work following on the lesson.
10. Suitable conditions are essential for good broadcast lessons.
11. Permanent machinery is needed to secure continuous contact between B.B.C. on the one hand, and on the other hand, the Board of Education, Local Education Authorities and the whole body of teachers.
12. Secondary Schools have found the provisions hitherto made for them unsuitable. It is desirable that the B.B.C. should, after consulting with the schools, experiment with further types of courses.
13. The time was not ripe for a thorough test of Adult Education by wireless. The evidence available shows that the group system was to a certain extent successful, but that other methods should be investigated. The immediate need is for a more effective liaison between the B.B.C. and listeners and potential listeners.[1]

[1] "Educational Broadcasting." *Report of a Special Investigation in the County of Kent during the Year 1927.* The Carnegie United Kingdom Trustees, Comely Park House. Dunfermline, 1928.

Date Due

Demco 293-5			